THE 30 SOMETHING CEO

THE 30 SOMETHING CEO

DARK SECRETS AND
BRAVE METHODS OF THE
CORPORATE BATTLEFIELD

VINEET BAJPAI

JAICO PUBLISHING HOUSE

Ahmedabad Bangalore Chennai
Delhi Hyderabad Kolkata Mumbai

Published by Jaico Publishing House
A-2 Jash Chambers, 7-A Sir Phirozshah Mehta Road
Fort, Mumbai - 400 001
jaicopub@jaicobooks.com
www.jaicobooks.com

To be sold only in India, Bangladesh, Bhutan,
Pakistan, Nepal, Sri Lanka and the Maldives.

THE 30-SOMETHING CEO
ISBN 978-81-8495-820-1

First Jaico Impression: 2016

Page design and layout: Jojy Philip, Delhi

Printed by
Repro India Limited, Mumbai

To

Vedika, Aditi

&

Vandita

Contents

Acknowledgements

This is the third time I am getting to write the acknowledgement for a book, which gives me the third opportunity to thank mostly the same people. And I am delighted to be able to do this.

As I age from being a 26-year-old author of my first book *Build From Scratch*, to a 33-year-old writer of my second book, *The Street to the Highway* (and its Hindi translation *Aasmaan Se Aagey*), and now to being a 38-year-old writing veteran so to speak, I have realised something very precious. I realised that the people I want to thank today are largely the same as the ones I thanked twelve years ago, when *Build From Scratch* was released. What more can one ask for?

As always, the first set of people I want to express my deepest gratitude to is my team from my three companies – Talentrack,

Magnon eg+ and Magnon\TBWA. I take Talentrack's name first because it is the youngest, and needs a bit of pampering! The total number of people in these companies together runs into several hundreds and I cannot name everyone, but I am equally indebted to all of you. You are my business *militia*, my force, my confidence and my courage.

I have to take a few names because without these people I would not have enjoyed the knowledge or the authority to write this book or any other. Vivek Merani, Managing Director of Magnon eg+ and my friend for two decades, is my dearest and most dependable confidante. Vivek, you are my brother from another mother. Nitin Naresh, Managing Director of Magnon\TBWA, is someone I'd take a bullet for. And I know he will take one for me. Thanks so much, Nitin! Krishna Jha, Executive Director of Talentrack, you are a full-blooded battle soldier bro. We will conquer the world together. Prashant (or Sheelu as we lovingly call you), you are my partner in crime for three and a half decades now. I hope it stays like this for another few. Manishi Singh, my co-founder at Talentrack, I am fortunate to have found you, my friend. There is a lot we are destined to achieve together.

There are many more names from the Talentrack and Magnon families that I owe boundless gratitude to. Sunil Ahuja, Naved Aqueel, Vikas Misra, Joydeep Kalra, Jitentra Sawant, Ayush Gupta, Pratul Gaur, Denny Joseph, Siya Khanna, Sakhi Khanna, Jivak Davare, Hemant Nagar, Reena Singh, Chanda Sarma, Swati

Gupta, Jatin Madan, Pankaj Soni, Naveen Sharma, Jagdish Pant, Jitendra Kumar, Sankar Basu, Vikas Tiwari, Kavita Siddiqui, Sonu Bansal, Gurpreet Singh…to name a few. Thank you for everything guys!

My story would be incomplete without a heartfelt mention of the Omnicom, TBWA and eg+ Worldwide networks, where I have spent several years of invaluable learning, growth and rich exposure. I express my sincere gratitude to the following iconic and fantastic leaders of the Omnicom, TBWA and eg+ families – Troy Ruhanen (President & CEO, TBWA Worldwide), Denis Streiff (CFO, TBWA Worldwide), Paul Hosea (CEO, eg+ Worldwide), Simon Toaldo (President International, eg+ Worldwide), Alain Rhone (COO International, eg+ Worldwide), Keith Smith (President International, TBWA Worldwide), Philip Brett (President, TBWA Asia), Emmanuel Andre (President International, TBWA Worldwide), Dara Akbarian (CFO, APAC, Omnicom Group), Mark Rhys Thomas (Chief Strategy Officer, eg+ Worldwide), Darren Jackson (CFO, TBWA Asia), Ramzi Raad (Group Chairman, TBWA\RAAD), Reda Raad (CEO, TBWA\RAAD), Neeraj Puri (Director, Omnicom India) and Paul Fothergill (CFO, eg+ Worldwide). Thank you all for being my greatest mentors and for supporting me at every step.

I am fortunate to have the encouragement of some extraordinary people in my life, who have had a profound impact on me and my career. I will not miss this opportunity to thank them. Nishish Jha, Founder & Managing Partner,

Unigrowth Canada Inc., for trusting me and for investing in Talentrack when it was just an idea. Asheesh Khanna, Chairman, SISAR, for betting on me the second time. Navin Chawla (Navin Uncle), Former Chief Election Commissioner of India, for being an infinite source of inspiration. My dear friend and National Spokesperson of the Samajwadi Party, Gaurav Bhatia, for loving me selflessly despite all my silly whims. You are a true idol for India's youth Gaurav. Anil Shastriji and Dr. GL Sharma, Lal Bahadur Shastri Institute of Management, for giving me more affection than anyone expects from his *alma mater*. This is my ninth year as the President of our powerful alumni association. Thank you! And Praveen Puri, for hand-holding me into the world of academia and writing.

This section would be incomplete until I write about *Guruji*, Sri Sri Ravi Shankar (Art of Living). I have met you in-person only once Guruji, but the impression will remain etched on my mind, heart and soul always. You are a true *sanyasi* and I pray to God that I get more opportunities to be by your side.

The Jaico family, my publisher, is a glaring example of what successful companies should be like. They are one of the oldest and most respected publishing houses in India, but work with the sincerity and humility of a start-up. Akash Shah, thank you for being a friend and partner as we release our third book together. Vijay Thakur, you are the one who makes sure my books reach thousands of readers. Thank you very much!

If I even begin to express how much my family means to me

and what role they have played in my journey, I will end up writing a whole book. I think they know. They know my very existence is powered by their love.

Success & spirit

Vineet Bajpai

> “How great are the dangers I face, to win a good name in Athens
>
> – Alexander the Great

introduction

I have spent 17 years on the corporate battleground. And I don't use the term 'battleground' just for melodrama. It has been a battleground in perhaps every sense. Also, more than just the time that has passed, I can safely say that it is the rigour and intensity of the journey that has been the highlight of these years. Bankruptcy, office-sealing, client walk-outs, betrayal, public slander, sunk investments, sour deals, gangsters, failed business plans, mergers & acquisitions, crushing loans, litigation, multinational corporate politics....there is very little that I have not been through over the years. Some people call it madness to withstand such sustained and insufferable pressures, for so many years continuously. I call it the price I have paid for *'a good name in Athens'*.

I am the Founder & CEO of Talentrack – India's leading mobile & web platform for media, entertainment, creative & art talent-hiring. I am also the Chairman of the Magnon Group. Before this, I was the Group CEO of the TBWA \ India, one of the largest multinational advertising corporations in the world. And even before that, I founded and built Magnon, one of the biggest digital media companies in Asia. I am 38.

So while I still have many miles to travel – I *am* a *30-something CEO.*

This book is not about me. It is about you. It is about who you are today, and who you are going to become tomorrow. It is a bold enquiry into why and how some people become exceedingly successful at whatever they do, and why most others fail miserably. It is a debate and an instruction manual about how we all are the writers as well as the vehicles of our own destinies. Eventually, it is a deafening appeal to you – take the reins of your future in your own hands. Now!

Let's start with a set of questions. These might disturb you, or might awaken you:

- ➢ What are your ambitions and what defines them?
- ➢ Where do you see yourself on the social and corporate ladder a few years from now, and why?
- ➢ If you are just starting-out in your career, how do you

plan to outpace and outperform your peers and win the race towards the corner office? What are you doing to prepare yourself for this long and hard competitive journey? Do you think your degree will be enough?

- Do you believe that you will find a way as life unfolds itself? Do you really think it is going to be that easy?
- If you are already deep into your working life, what career-progression have you accepted as your *fait accompli*, and why?
- Have you given up on the dream of becoming a multi-millionaire?
- Have you started to believe that you have only one-in-a-million chances of becoming the CEO of a global company?
- Worst of all, have you stopped making grand plans and stopped seeing spectacular dreams for yourself, your life and your career?
- In short, have you quit being that dreamy-eyed, *'I will get what I want'* college kid you were just a few years back? Or do you still have a burning furnace in your belly, but don't know what to do with it?

If the answers to the above questions are more yes than no, I am here to shake you back into top-gear and to get you into that dreamy-eyed zone again – and this time, with significantly more achievement-arsenal.

> Life grants nothing to us mortals without hard work.
>
> – Horace

Remember this – for winners, time is like high-octane fuel. It drives them on - relentlessly, unstoppably. But for the mediocre, time is like rust – slow, static, inevitable and degenerative. Almost all of us start our careers, businesses and lives burning with hope, belief and dreams. Then, five years pass by. Half of us get scorched in the fire of reality and tone our aspirations down a few notches. Another five years pass by. By then, almost all of us have accepted lives and careers far inferior to what we expected from ourselves when we started out. Why? What goes wrong?

I think I know what goes wrong.

You. *You go wrong.*

In my years as an employee of a mammoth multinational, in my years as a start-up entrepreneur, as a growing company promoter, a management lecturer, a business and inspirational writer, a corporate CEO and a motivational speaker, I have enjoyed the rare opportunity of observing and working with a wide spectrum of people. I have been able to spot trends, to identify a common and predictable thread of destiny repeating itself, mistakes being made over and over again, fundamentals of winning forgotten, people blaming the world and everything around them for their failures, ambition in words but not in actions, desire becoming common but sacrifice becoming rare, a general loss of direction as well as that of a fierce quest for success. And it will be my sincere endeavour to elucidate all of these, and to forewarn you about them. I will also try and guide you towards launching a massive individual counter-attack against these dangerous, career-corroding, yet common phenomena.

I will try not to let you go wrong again. I will try to prepare you to become a *30-something CEO*. From here on, we are together in this.

My own struggles, limitations, self-doubts, perseverance, weaknesses, failures, and eventual triumphs have taught me a few invaluable lessons – and I can say that I am now a student of a well-documented but rarely practised way-of-life, a mantra for winning, a framework for victory. In short, I am privy to some secrets that all of us need to unfurl and embrace. I will share these secrets, this art, this intense craft with you through the next few pages. But again, I have also learnt one very crucial and bitter truth – that while all of us dream, hope and talk of that much-awaited 'dawn' in our lives, it is an unnervingly small fraction of us that are willing to pay the price for that beautiful morning. To understand what I am saying a little better, let us start from where we all normally start our careers – from the *bindaas* days of our university colleges, our professional institutes and our business schools.

Remember conversations over *samosas* with buddies in the college canteen, when we were young and barely a few steps away from our working lives? *"I will buy that fashionable car by the time I am 25 years of age,"* one friend would say. Another would add, *"I will own that swanky apartment in Noida before I am 30"*. And almost all of them would say the one thing I have heard so many times in my working life – ***"I will be a CEO while I am still in my thirties"***. A bold, almost arrogant statement.

Being *the 30-something CEO* is like a badge that describes perhaps the most coveted dream for the contemporary youth of India. It represents many things. It embodies the aspirations of a new and ambitious generation. It shows a significant growth in the corporate sector and the industry, in a country where it was the state that represented successful careers till as recently as even the previous generation. It characterizes a people in a rush – people who want the very best in life, and want it before they are old and grey. It shows belief, confidence and clear goal-identification. It is almost the tacit war slogan for a country and an economy that is on rapid ascent. Readers who are not from the corporate sector should not take the term CEO as specific to the industry. The term CEO denotes reaching the heights of success in whatever career you choose. This is very important to understand as I have used the term *30-something CEO* probably a hundred times or more in this book. So it could be a 30-something entrepreneur, or a 30-something Supreme Court senior advocate, or a 30-something Lieutenant Colonel – as long as the aim and the meaning signifies unquestioned and unusual success.

Also, please note that this book is not *only* about the 30-something people or people in their teens and twenties.

The term 30-something is a metaphor to denote exceptional success. If you are a reader in your forties or fifties, please don't be disheartened or disconnected. Becoming a 52-year-old CEO is an equally terrific and rare achievement, given the statistics of how many people actually reach that height. Moreover, the fundamental spirit we all need to carry is to strive for success irrespective of where we are in our career, how old we happen to be or how difficult our circumstances are. Colonel Harland Sanders was 61 when he started the KFC franchise. Khushwant Singh wrote a bestseller at 96. For me, they are both *30-something CEOs*. This book is about dreamers, who know age cannot be a parameter. This book is about believers, who know that ambition knows no excuses.

And it is not wrong to have this ambition. The corporate sector and the world at large have changed for the better – in favour of the performer, the fighter. While CEOs were conventionally supposed to be in their late fifties or sixties, or early fifties at best, stories of extraordinary achievers leading massive companies at 37 or 38 years of age are not totally uncommon today. Companies are spotting talent faster, rewarding performers and putting a premium on youthful leadership. Becoming a CEO today is not only a factor dependant on the number of decades one has spent in the industry or the corporation, but also on path-breaking leadership, on the ability to forge and execute strategies, and on showing measurable output. Today's CEO is not just about experience. He is about results.

So the *30-something CEO* dream is a real symbol of hope for millions of children in their teens, twenties and early-thirties. Given that India is a young-nation with a majority of our population below 35, we are talking about an enormous number of people here.

So all is well, right? The dream, the hope, the desire, the ambition and most of all – the opportunities... everything is in place, correct? *Nahin yaar*. Not quite.

Why are millions of people feeling like under-achievers today? Why are their hopes defeated? Why does a very large majority of us feel we could have done much better than what we are doing? Why are we still staring at that fashionable SUV from our motorcycles, metro trains or economy cars? Why are we still living in rented apartments or paying back-breaking loan instalments? Why do we still read the right-hand column of the menu in a remotely expensive restaurant? We are about to become *30-something CEOs*. CEOs don't go through this grind! What the hell happened? *Again, what went wrong?*

> The world needs dreamers and the world needs doers. But above all, the world needs dreamers who do.
>
> – Sarah Ban Breathnach

There is nothing more corrosive than a dream without determination; than hope without hard-work; than ambition without the willingness to give all you have. And except for the super-achievers of this world since time immemorial, we all suffer from this syndrome. Our parents and teachers taught us to be ambitious; but no one told us what ambition demands! They told us to aim for the stars; but we got no education on where to get the rocket-fuel for the journey! As our greatest well-wishers, they encouraged us to win; but never told us what winning will take away! The system trained us to work towards milestones – exams, tests, selections, interviews etc., but no one disclosed that winning in life is not about milestones – it is about traversing the road tirelessly, unstoppably, unflappably. Till the very last breath.

We talk, we hope, we daydream. We forget that *dawn* when things are easy and we remember it again when life gives us a jolt. We desire it when insulted; we flaunt it when ambitious talk is the order of the day; we assume that our day-of-success will happen sometime; we label winners as 'lucky'; we feel the years of work will eventually bring that much-deserved corporate achievement our way and so on. We keep waiting, hoping, dreaming, talking...

...failing, tiring and ageing. With every passing day.

Scary but true.

But some of us win, right? Some of us keep the hope alive for everyone. These winners sparkle like the North Star, they bend rules, they live the dreams we all had for ourselves. You will see that one-among-a-thousand boys from your college batch became a corporate tycoon. There is always this one girl who broke the shackles of conventional career-progression and today drives her red Porsche to her corner office in that glass tower. You keep seeing this neighbourhood friend you had in your childhood, now featuring on magazine covers. *How did they do it?*

This book will tell you how.

This book will help you avoid the inconspicuous yet very potent mediocrity trap that millions around us are falling into. It will remind you of your dreams, reawaken them, and then show you how much effort, sacrifice and sustained commitment would be needed to achieve what you want. Eventually, it will hand-hold you and push you towards all that you need to harness mentally, physically, emotionally and spiritually – to become *the 30-something CEO.*

Welcome to the dark secrets and the brave methods of the winners.

> “There’s nowhere you can be that isn’t where you’re meant to be.
>
> – John Lennon

are you the one?

Global CEO or retired senior manager – What is your destiny?

Every multinational corporation, every large enterprise, every big business house employs thousands of people at any given time. With several offices, numerous manufacturing or service delivery units, mammoth budgets, variety of geographies, millions of retail customers or scores of corporate clients, lawyers, bankers, accountants... *they have only one CEO.* To put it in the right perspective, this is the simplest way of concluding that a CEO is one in thousands, sometimes tens of thousands. A simple corollary would mean that only one out of ten thousand people in the fray will actually make it to the top. Not very friendly odds I must say. This is true not just for the CEO's seat alone. This is true for any winning position – it could be the CFO or COO of a multinational corporation, senior partner in a law firm, the national head of sales, the national creative director of an advertising agency, the vice chancellor of a university or absolutely any coveted profile that promises the prosperity, influence and fame that we all desire to achieve.

The convenient oblivion

How did you start your career? As a Management Trainee from a reputed B-school, or a hard-working graduate who made his way up the corporate ladder, slowly but steadily? Did you start as a software engineer who is now looking after a business team, or as a field sales executive who is now the territory manager? Whatever position you may have started from, please let me tell you how much I respect you. It is not easy to find a place, big or small, in today's hard and ruthless world. If you have succeeded in finding even a small spot for yourself, you deserve appreciation.

Now for some hard-hitting questions.

- Do you think, at your speed, you will make it as big as you always thought you would?
- Are you galloping towards the dream you started out

to achieve, or do you sometimes suspect that you are not really moving in the direction or with the speed that will take you to your goal?

- Most importantly, do you even have a well-defined, clearly visible career target? Or are you moving in a general career drift, ready to accept whatever life may throw your way as the years pass by and your hair turn grey?

Look around you. You will find a few success stories. Look again – now, with a different perspective. How many stories of failures or mediocrities do you notice? It sometimes bewilders me as to how we spot and get awed by the winners, but don't notice the thousands of failures that co-exist around us.

> Day after day countless people die. Yet the living hopes to live forever. O Lord, what can be a greater wonder?
>
> – Yudhisthira, The Mahabharata

That close-to-retirement uncle who now lives a very middle-class life and takes the train to his office everyday wearing his decade old sweater – was also a strapping 27-year-old at one time, totally confident that he would retire in a mansion with a Mercedes. He won't. Do you think that the aged, irritable admin officer in your organisation foresaw or chose his destiny that ended up as a mediocre executive? He didn't. Even that seemingly successful senior manager is perhaps nowhere close to where he hoped to get. He thought he would become a global CEO. But he won't. He would retire as the senior manager. Good, but not even remotely great.

Every family, every neighbourhood, every office is flooded with the 'also-rans', the guys who got left behind, the people who missed the bus.

We see them, but we don't take notice. We feel the same would never happen to us.

It will. To most of us.

Unless we change something... *NOW.*

Most of us live in a strange yet convenient oblivion. We loosen our grip over our lives and allow destiny to take over rather than shaping it ourselves. We watch a limited overs cricket match and keep a close track of the run-rate. We map the runs needed to win against the bowling overs that remain. We do this for a game on TV. But we forget to do this very basic exercise for something as defining as our own careers. We don't track years, we don't give ourselves an annual performance report, we don't identify the exact winning goal nor the distance from it... we just let life roll by... month after month, year after year. We think that going to work every day and doing our routine jobs will take us to that shining moment of success. Till we discover ourselves in a train, wearing that decade-old sweater to work. Or find ourselves in the old senior manager's cubicle, at 58… angry with everything.

We let mediocrity happen to us! It never takes anyone by surprise. At a sub-conscious level, we all know something is not right. We all know that the master-plan is going haywire. Yet, we use every single weekend to watch movies and sprawl in front of the TV – but never to shut ourselves in a room to rigorously examine our lives and careers.

The *30-something CEO* does nothing like that.

> Rich people have small TVs and big libraries, and poor people have small libraries and big TVs.
>
> \- Zig Ziglar

So wherever you are in your career, I think it might be a good idea to pause and evaluate your progress so far. If you are a student about to enter the real battlefield, you are in a position of great advantage. You can start with an extra dose of nitro from day one. You can plan your offensive at the most micro level from the very beginning. For all of us in our work-lives already, it is time we think what our ultimate goal is. Or was! What are you working for? What do you dream to become? I am very certain that the original blueprint of your life and career as per you, was not about barely earning a middle-class living. It was a greater dream. The problem is, you don't dream it that often now. The problem is, you have let life guide your expectations rather than it being the other way round.

What we sometimes forget is that extraordinary corporate growth, or for that matter success in any field, does not just happen as you spend years going to office. Yes, some natural or organic growth does trickle in as one spends years on a job, but we must not forget that these years are very limited. Taking an average age of 23 to start one's career and an average age of 63 for retirement, we only have forty laps in the race. Doesn't sound like too much time when put this way, right? For many of us reading these lines, a smaller yet significant part of the journey might already be behind us. So we have to accelerate, gain momentum and deliver spectacular performance in the next few years, so as to not only win the race – but to win it by a long margin.

And that will not happen till we break-free from the convenient but deadly oblivion surrounding us. It will not happen till we wake up.

A board-meeting with yourself

Most of us are used to it – call it a board meeting, a sales review, a performance evaluation or an appraisal interview. We are OK with such regime being a part of our lives. How can our superiors or organisations assess us unless they question us, grill us and subject us to some hard scrutiny, right? Perhaps, yes. So you are ready and willing to get scanned for every action and every success/failure at work when someone else is forcing you for the same? But when was the last time you evaluated yourself? When was the last time you assigned grades to yourself on critical life and career parameters like focus, result-orientation, discipline, vision, fitness, enterprise, and commitment? You let others evaluate you and your capabilities, but you completely forget to forge your life-armour under the furnace of your own ambition and grit?

Why?

> Attack the evil that is within yourself, rather than attacking the evil that is in others.
>
> \- Confucius

You've got to get this one point I am trying to make here crystal clear. You cannot expect to achieve extraordinary success if you like to live your life like an ordinary person. It is a hard, perhaps scary statement to make, but it is the truth. *Success demands sacrifice.*

I think it is only about now that we have reached the real buzzword – sacrifice. And equally important – realisation. I can never forget a few scenes from the blockbuster movie 'The Matrix' – where Morpheus (played by Laurence Fishburne) gives Neo (played by Keanu Reeves) a choice between two pills – red and blue. One would make him forget all the new discoveries he has made and take him back to the slumber of the Matrix. The other would take him to awakening in the real world. Harder but truer.

Neo chooses the pill that takes him to reality. Because like they say in the movie – *He is The One.*

> Remember: all I am offering is the truth, nothing more.
>
> – Morpheus, The Matrix

The truth is that most of us have allowed ourselves to get lost in the maze and the comfortable confusion of this hard world. Instead of making our way through the thorny path of this jigsaw puzzle, we choose to declare to ourselves at a subconscious level that the world is too complicated for us to make an impact. Well, the truth is, it is not. Nearly everything that happens to you, good or bad, is an outcome of a seed sown by you, years ago. People suffer from high cholesterol and get medical help for it. But the cholesterol did not get built because of this morning's breakfast. It was allowed to flourish over years of convenient indiscipline. A student fails in his annual examination. But it was not a result of last evening's movie plan. It was something that he knew somewhere deep down was going to happen. It was convenient avoidance of the reality. Similarly, when we underperform in our lives and careers, it is not an outcome of what we did or failed to do this week, this month or this year. It is a cumulative result of what we have been doing or not doing over the years. It is like the cholesterol. It is the convenient oblivion we allow ourselves to live in.

•❖•

I am quite confident that by now you would have grasped the message I am trying to send across. Stop waiting for success. Start running towards it. The first step towards extraordinary growth is being conscious of every passing day and knowing that time is ticking away in its usual blaze, whether you take notice or not. It is being aware that every hour of hard work and smart work that you put in over and above what your contemporaries do, accelerates your speed towards your ultimate goal. And most importantly, it is in reminding yourself every day that success will turn and smile at you only when you step out and scream out for it. That scream made from the decibels of your sweat and toil. From your feverish and indomitable will to win!

Your destiny is in your very own hands. In the few waking hours of every single day. We will talk about more granular and clearer execution measures towards your goal as we move forward in this book. But every great journey has to start with the absolute commitment of the traveller.

You need to live for your dream – before you can live your dream.

> "I hated every minute of training, but I said "Don't quit. Suffer now and live the rest of your life as a champion".
>
> – Muhammad Ali

the rabbit that didn't rest

The work-life balance seekers, the vacation-lovers...*and the winners who give everything*

Ever thought what would have been the outcome of the well-known 'rabbit & tortoise' race if the rabbit had chosen *not* to take that nap? If he had decided to press on, despite the long margin he was winning by, he would have won the race by a distance that was unbeatable. The problem is, he *did* take that nap. And he lost for reasons that were his own. His own choices.

During one of my media interviews, about a year ago, the beautiful and sharp journalist asked me how I find time to write business books despite my crippling work schedule as the CEO of Talentrack, and as CEO of other companies prior to that. Simply and honestly, I gave her a six-word reply – *'I don't watch movies on weekends'*. Even today, I don't know why she threw her head back and laughed out loud, and re-enquired, *Nahin yaar, seriously!*' She found my answer either too boring, too bereft of the management *gyan* she was probably expecting, or unbelievable. But it was true. I meant it. I remembered the innumerable times I refused my closest friends for a great movie, a fine dinner or a fun day out – just because I wanted to use a good four hours to write. It came to me naturally and it did not come that easily to that feature writer. She ignored that part of the interview and it never found a place in what was published two days later. But it was true. I meant it.

The worst of both worlds?

Sometimes, I worry that while we have imbibed some very productive habits and lifestyles from the West (and vice versa – given the Yoga, Infotech and more!), have we somewhere concocted a botched-up career-formula for ourselves? Before I say anything more, let me please confess and remind you that my own first professional chapter was written in the sunny atrium of

General Electric, a fantastic American company. Two of my finest mentors were an Englishman and a Frenchman. One of my closest business partners is Lebanese and we work closely in the United Arab Emirates. New York and Hong Kong are two of my favourite business cities, and Rome is my perfect holiday destination. So I am as globally connected or 'infected' as anyone can be. And I am proud of it. This invaluable exposure has taught me more than what I learnt for a decade in school.

Yet, I say I am worried about the rapid and sometimes even blind emulation of the West we, Indians have started introducing in our daily lives. We forget that the reason why Americans feel threatened by the Indians and the Chinese is because we are willing to work harder and longer than they are. We are ready to work on Diwali, Christmas, during Hanukkah, and even on New Year's Eve. We are ready to work on Sundays, at nights, on holidays... all, without complaining. And that is because we belong to resurgent economies. We are fighting and gradually shedding the baggage of under-development and colonization from the previous century. We need to try harder. And that is why we are global forces to reckon with today. But are we going to let that fighting-spirit change at the very first sign of economic progress? At both personal and collective levels?

I have witnessed a shift in my own career. The proud Indian statement, *'We offer our services 24x7x365'*, is swiftly giving way to the *'I work four and a half days a week'* Indian professional. Please don't get me wrong. I am not objecting to people taking time out for family and leisure. It is important, healthy and must not be ignored. But there is a Sanskrit saying that goes, '*Ati sarvatra varjayeta*', meaning, the extremity of anything should be discarded/prohibited. Are we really at a place where we can start tuning out on a Friday afternoon to remember our work again only on Monday morning? Do we not need to run that extra mile both as a nation and as individual dreamers? We have made progress but are still many, many miles away from our spectacular goals. Why are we slowing down, when we need to accelerate the most?

All this while we have been talking about *The 30-something CEO*, about the extraordinary achiever. What about the *extra* in extraordinary? Where is the *extra*? If we take that away, we are left with just... *ordinary.*

In the previous chapter, I had mentioned that success demands sacrifice. It takes more than an ordinary or routine or *this-is-what-everyone-does* approach. We ape the Americans in the way they take their annual vacations. But, we forget that they have social security to look after them in their hour of need. We like to frolic away our weekends like the Australians, without remembering the abundance they enjoy in terms of opportunities and lifestyle. Most of us have forgotten how we have been trained to study at night and grab those extra few hours on a Saturday, to get ahead of our school and college mates. It came naturally to us then, and has been the gritty Indian way of pushing the boundaries. It has worked for us. We have emerged from the dark shadows of mass poverty and starvation, to transform into a global economic power. Even at an individual level, we see how our lifestyles and comforts have witnessed radical advancement. Why are we then slowing down now? Why are weekends, holidays and the movies suddenly dominating our lives? *The 30-something CEO* takes holidays too. But fewer than most others. More well-deserved than the others.

We have not reached the goal. We have not come even close to our dreams. So, then why do we nap every now and then like the complacent rabbit?

Getting it right – rabbit speed + tortoise perseverance

> Genius is 1% talent and 99% hard work.
>
> – Albert Einstein

Rabbits, tortoises… yes, I know this is beginning to sound like *Jataka* tales! But then, who said these were not the best sources of worldly wisdom? Let's go through some simple examples to elucidate why I am snatching you away from your weekend revelry and your love for the cinemas.

I read somewhere that Sachin Tendulkar practiced playing cricket non-stop for so many hours a day, every day, that he would invariably drop off to sleep on the dining table. The legendary author Jeffrey Archer said in an interview that he writes every day. Yes, every day. Andre Agassi hit 2,500 tennis balls in a single day at a home-made court at the age of six! Practice, discipline, sacrifice... what else do you think forges champions and winners? Do you think a regular Joe with a regular daily and weekly routine can become a shining star in the competitive blue sky of the corporate universe, if he continues on the same path? I don't think so.

> Success is never owned, it is rented. And the rent is due every day.
>
> – Rory Vaden

Let's understand this really clearly. No one in his right senses would suggest that you over-work yourself and burn-out. It is now, thankfully, an accepted fact that our brain and our nervous system are as vulnerable to wear and tear as our bones and muscles. The brain tires. The nervous system needs care. Anxiety, depression, lack of concentration, chronic stress... all these are quite commonplace in today's fiercely demanding environment. So you have to grasp this section very carefully and pick-up what suits you most. Like everything else in life, it is balance that works best here. The only debate is, what *is* the right balance?

I have led several companies in the last seventeen years of my career. It has given me the opportunity to work with all sorts and species of the corporate animal – the flamboyant achiever, the mad creative genius, the dull sales-star, the all-talk-no-walk boss-pleaser and more. I am fortunate to have worked with some of them, as they have been precious teachers and great friends. But these years have also given me the opportunity to closely observe, perhaps hundreds and thousands of young professionals. While I have not maintained mathematical data-charts, there is a clear trend I have noticed over the years – that those who delivered the least results, were the ones that asked for most breaks! And, the one that were spectacular performers, were those that took holidays sparingly. At least, till they reached a certain level of seniority and professional establishment. Some of the real champions I have worked with are people who I have had to literally push out of the office! And it is true for all rungs and tiers. A junior accountant in my company amazes me with his undying commitment and sheer slogging. I know he will be a star one day. Soon.

So why does such a phenomenon take place? Why does the achiever reward himself less, while the under-performer maintains a log of the minutest details of his leave entitlement? I know of a 28-year-old in my company who signs in sick on a month-closing Friday, and posts rock-climbing photographs on Instagram the following Sunday! On the other hand, I work with this brilliant digital marketing manager who keeps her very-accommodating husband waiting in the office parking lot while she is analysing online consumer-conversations about her client-brand, late at night. As I write this, she is due for a fast-track promotion. The rock-climber… err… well, he can climb the Everest with all the free time I think he will have on his hands, very soon.

> There is no substitute for hard work.
>
> – Thomas A Edison

Wait a minute...are we studying the wrong end of the corollary? Is it the performer who takes less holidays, or is it the other way round? Does the winner devote himself more, or the one who devotes himself more, wins? Have I been observing the trend upside-down all these years? I think the answer is yes.

Let's take the question to you. What do you see around you? How many friends, colleagues or family-members do you have around you, who impress and inspire you with their commitment to their work and goals? I can tell you there wouldn't be too many. In fact, some of you may not have even one such torch-bearer in your immediate circle. You will find several friends who plan road-trips, beer-afternoons and beach-holidays, but do you also have someone you know who epitomizes hard-work, sacrifice and a bit of genius (which is often a by-product of the first two)? Probably not. And that is because there *are* so very few of them. Those rare gems, those history-creators... those winners. And that is why there is only one *30-something CEO* among thousands of ordinary people.

Most of us are familiar with the *Mahabharata* – the great epic. As one may recall, the valiant and virtuous *Pandava* brothers are sent into exile after a humiliating defeat against the *Kaurava* brothers at *chausad*, an ancient form of gambling. Most of us would know that the *Pandavas* suffered a long forest exile and came back to wage a mammoth war for the victory of good over evil. But a question that very few of us would have pondered over however, is that what did the *Pandavas* actually *do* during these thirteen years of banishment. Well, I can tell you with my limited knowledge of the epics that four of the *Pandava* brothers and their wife, *Draupadi* spent those years in a bitter wait for retribution. But what did the fifth *Pandava* – the great archer *Arjuna*, do during these years? Did he rest? Did he simply while away time waiting for the exile to get over? No, he did not. At the counsel of his friend and cousin Lord *Krishna* himself, Arjuna spent those years in hard penance and in an insatiable quest for *divyaastras*, or divine weapons of mass destruction. He travelled to far lands, he fought demons and Gods, and he transformed himself into the most skilled and feared warrior in the then known world. So, while the Kauravas and the other Pandavas spent these thirteen years in what they knew to be the lull before the storm, Arjuna actually built an impregnable armour of dedication, discipline, humility and talent around him.

Little wonder then that it was Arjuna who almost single-handedly won the greatest war on the face of the Earth, and established the rule of *Dharma* or righteousness. And he is remembered and revered by nearly a billion people even today, as the most magnificent warrior to have ever walked this planet.

He was *a 30-something CEO* in circa 2500 BC.

I urge you to find the Arjuna within you. To know that while we don't fight modern-day corporate battles with swords and arrows, there are the victors and the vanquished even today. Penance may have to take the form of intense hard-work; *divyaastras* maybe the new technical and managerial skills... but the rules of the game stand unchanged. Even today only Arjuna wins.

> You have to fight to reach your dream. You have to sacrifice and work hard for it.
>
> \- Lionel Messi

I know what you must be thinking. On the one hand, this guy is telling me how important it is to balance work and health, and on the other, he is asking me to break my back and make sacrifices. Well, what can I say. You have understood it right. I *am* asking you to do this. Sachin Tendulkar was perhaps the longest-playing international cricketer in the history of the game. Those of us who have read about him and observed his rise closely, would know of the intensity of his commitment, his gruelling regimen and his unparalleled devotion to the sport. Yet, to the disappointment of his billion loving fans, every now and then, he would skip a one-day series or a test-match. So, while he pushed the boundaries of this great sport beyond what anyone else could do before him, he also gave his mind and body the rest that was required for him to stay on the top for over two decades. We will all have to find the same mix of determination and pace in our lives and careers.

Let your professional conscience be your primary advisor. Don't take a break unless you are convinced that you need one. But once you are convinced, don't hold yourself back. Use those extra hours to grow your skills, or to network and to learn… do grab that beer and movie when you really feel the need for rejuvenation. But, for God's sake, don't work solely for the shallow purpose of having fun with what you earn. Don't work for the weekend. Work to achieve greatness. Work towards becoming *the 30-something CEO.*

> When you walk up to opportunity's door... don't knock it. Kick that bitch in. Smile and introduce yourself.
>
> – Dwayne 'The Rock' Johnson

warriors win, not weapons

So what if you don't have the degree from that fancy institute?

Richard Branson was told by his school principal that he would either end up in prison or as a millionaire. Sir Branson did not accumulate any high degrees thereafter. We all know where he ended-up. Steve Jobs dropped out of college to travel to India and learn Buddhism. Dhirubhai Ambani had little formal education and worked as a petrol pump attendant. Bill Gates dropped out of Harvard. Warren Buffet was rejected by Harvard. Need I say more?

Head-start yes, Endgame no

One of the most commonly shared perceptions about fast-track corporate success is that those 'lucky' few super-achievers are people with ivy-league degrees from world-class institutions. And once we have missed the bus in the early stages of our careers, there is no way we can compete or catch-up with them. Some newspaper stories about spectacular starting salaries being offered by companies like Google and Microsoft to a few young pass-outs from an IIT or an IIM somehow reaffirm that widespread belief. As a result, we accept a second-grade corporate citizen status for ourselves at a sub-conscious level. In other words, we declare ourselves defeated even before the race begins.

There is no doubt or debate about the head-start and propulsion a brilliant degree from a premier institution provides. And we should not look at it as some kind of an undue advantage. Most people who get into these temples of learning are those front-row geeks who burnt the midnight oil and dug into their books, when most of us were texting boyfriends and girlfriends or watching TV for hours at length. So let's not take it away from them. They started before us. They started better than us.

But then, who said a superior start guarantees a superior end? Watch any sport and you will observe that while a good beginning definitely sets the match up in favour of the better-starter, by no means does it ensure a win. Haven't we seen great comebacks by sporting legends in epic games of tennis, cricket or football, or just about any sport, for that matter? The good thing about winning is that it takes a long time and is a hard-journey. And that journey is a great leveller. Success does not come in one quick catapult action. It comes with slow, harsh, punishing... days, months and years. Long evenings or early mornings spent in the solitude of your desk, with no one watching, no one appreciating and when there is no immediate gratification in sight. It takes the very determined, the very committed to continue treading that path for years together. And that is the good thing about success.

Let me make a confession. While I have an honours degree in Economics from one of the finest colleges in Delhi University, coupled with an MBA from a top-20 B-school, I did feel the absence of a Stanford or Wharton or Yale or an IIM stamp on myself during the early years of my career. I somehow felt inferior to anyone who came flashing these badges, and I don't think I was alone in that boat. But it was the grind of one and a half decades that taught me one precious lesson – better shoes can only take you so far in a race. They cannot make you win. Winning comes from within, not without.

Today, my companies have dozens of brilliant and capable professionals from the most premier institutions of the country working with us. *That* is the good thing about success.

The first three years...

> It is never too late to be who you might have been.
>
> - George Eliot

I vividly remember a funny and interesting incident that happened with me and one of my colleagues, several years ago. I had hired him for an important position post a long and grilling interview. About a year later, we happened to be on a flight together. During a conversation he mentioned something complicated about chemistry and I asked him how he knew so much about the subject. He turned to me with an almost shocked expression, asking, *'Vineet, don't you remember? I am a B.Tech in chemical engineering.'* I simply told him that I didn't remember, because I never knew about it in the first place! Then he reminded me of our long interview and wondered how I didn't remember. I couldn't help but laugh and tell him that I never even looked at his educational qualifications! He was being hired for a client-facing role and came with an excellent track record. I was only interested in the work he had done in his previous company(s) and how that would benefit us. He looked slightly disappointed, but agreed and understood fully nevertheless.

Why didn't I look at his educational degrees' column when I spent over two hours with him? Well, simply because looking at qualifications as a recruitment filter is the job of the guy who gives you your first job. At that time, he has no other real parameters to evaluate you on, and hence the degrees you bring to the table matter. But after that it is only what you do and deliver in the industry in the form of real and measurable results that counts. Now think about it...how absurd would it be for someone to hire an experienced investment banker on the grounds of his management degree in finance, when he has nothing concrete to show in terms of achievements in the real world? Would anyone hire a senior marketing professional just because he has a degree from IIM Ahmedabad, when he has no winning brand campaigns to talk about? Would you hire a seasoned salesman based on his sales diploma or on the proven sales numbers he has to display? The answers are obvious.

So what is important to understand here is that degrees do matter. Educational excellence certainly counts. Keeping aside the lifelong and well-deserved satisfaction that this excellence brings with it, in reality, practically, it counts in a big way for the first two, perhaps three, or maximum five years of your career. But that's just about it. Not beyond. After this early period of your career, it is your sustained and accepted organisational contribution, your reputation as a professional and your battleground performance that take over as the primary scales on which you are measured.

> "It's not who I am underneath, but what I do that defines me.
>
> – Batman *(Batman Begins)*

For those who already have an Ivy League education backing them, this should be a gentle cautionary note. It simply tells you that while their degrees are useful acceleration tools in the first lap of the race, they may not provide the same fuel in equal measure after that. And, even though they do have a well-earned lead in the quest towards becoming *the 30-something CEO*, there is no place for complacence. Beware the underdog who just ground his teeth.

> Out there in some garage is an entrepreneur who's forging a bullet with your company's name on it.
>
> – Gary Hamel

For those of us who do not have this advantage, the way forward is clear. It is a path with more intense hours spent at work. It is a road with more potholes and that requires even more grit. But even before we embark upon that journey, it is critical that we begin to *believe*. Believe that we can outperform the ivy league boys and girls. Believe that life is a long and serpentine track, where one temporary victory or defeat does not change the entire course and outcome of the journey. Believe that even now you have all that is needed to build a winning career for yourself. Believe that you are the next *30-something CEO*.

Now go back to the first paragraph of this chapter. Read again about Richard Branson, Steve Jobs, Dhirubhai Ambani, Warren

Buffet and Bill Gates. And it's not just them. Look around yourself. When you look hard enough you will realize that most of today's industry captains, most successful entrepreneurs, majority of the young super-achievers, are where they are at this point because of what they have delivered, and not what they had studied.

> 85% of your financial success is due to your personality and ability to communicate, negotiate and lead.
>
> Shockingly, only 15% is due to technical knowledge.
>
> – Carnegie Institute of Technology

As we move from the more inspirational content of this book to the on-ground and execution-oriented sections, there are several tactics and methods I will share with you, for you to shift your ambitions and achievements into top-gear and take on the toughest competitors in the business. Before I do so, however, it is absolutely imperative that you rise in your own mind and belief-system, and imagine yourself at the start-line with the highest-calibre talent in the industry.

You can't beat them till you believe you can.

Imagination rules the world.

– Napoleon Bonaparte

"they will never climb the mountain"

How start-ups and young companies can be your defining warfare tactic

"They will never climb the mountain..." or *"They can never cross the desert..."* have been among the famous last words of military Generals who lost epic battles – simply because they could not believe someone would have the courage or the determination to take a route they imagined to be insurmountable. It was people like T.E. Lawrence (*Lawrence of Arabia*) and Sir Horatio Nelson who changed the course of destiny by accomplishing what was unthinkable by their enemies. And that too by using methods that were not just considered unconventional, but actually insane to some degree.

There is a simple fact we need to grasp and internalise. Becoming a *30-something CEO* is not very highly probable if we follow the traditional, *walked-by-a-million-people* career-paths. I am sure you understand that something different, something special and something nearly crazy would be needed to provide the meteoric push that sets a few apart from the others. I know I have spoken much about commitment, hard-work and sacrifice in the previous chapters, and they remain critical to any success story. However, there is always inspiration that needs to partner the perspiration. That *enterprise* to accompany the hard-work. And it does not need to be some natural genius or talent that you are born with. It is something that we need to accept, learn and then implement as a well-planned career strategy. We will have to lead our professional lives with a penchant for not just spotting but creating opportunities. Not just going to work for many years and switching jobs once in a while, but living with enterprise, novelty and restless ambition as constant driving forces.

Let's take a look at the easy way of becoming a *30-something CEO*. Though I doubt this would be available to most of us.

I heard this joke a few years ago and I am tempted to share it with you here.

There was once a young and successful 32-year old professional named Raj, working for a large company. One day he was called-in into the Chairman's office. Once he had nervously settled down across the big mahogany desk, the Chairman began speaking, reading out Raj's achievements in just 5 years. He said, "Raj you joined us as an intern only five years ago. Within six months, you were promoted to an executive position. Then within just a year you became Senior Manager. You enjoyed rapid promotions to General Manager and then Vice President. And here you are today, ready to be appointed CEO of this company".

Raj sat there anxiously, waiting for the Chairman to complete.

After a few seconds the Chairman spoke again, "So Raj you do appreciate that you have witnessed extraordinary growth in this company. Do you have anything to say?"

Raj paused for a moment and said, "Thank you."

"Is that all you have to say?", thundered the Chairman.

Raj quickly corrected himself and said, "No I meant... thank you Dad".

So as the above little quip suggests, the quickest way to become a *30-something CEO* is when your family owns the company. And there is nothing wrong with that. Some of the finest business leaders of our times have been people who have inherited companies and businesses at a very young age, and led them to even greater heights. However, like I said, most of us are people whose families don't own businesses and companies. So this may not really be an option. But wait a minute. Can we not *create* some options for ourselves? Sure we can.

Let us now deep-dive into the real and practical methods that you can adopt to accelerate your journey and reach the CEO's corner cabin faster than all your professional and social competitors. Please let me forewarn you again, these methods will not be conventional. They may also not be absolutely novel. You might have probably thought about them and rejected them as unsuitable alternatives to your current trajectory. But I would urge you to read through them carefully, and give them a very serious thought. It could change the course of your life.

Method one - Entrepreneurship - The Guerrilla War

There is little doubt that all of us would have heard the term guerrilla-war. But do we know what guerrilla-war really means? To keep it simple, let me give you excerpts from the Wikipedia definition –

> *Guerrilla warfare is a form of irregular warfare in which a small group of combatants use military tactics*

including ambushes and mobility to fight a larger and less-mobile traditional military.

Now what does guerrilla warfare achieve? Why is it discussed and studied as an extremely effective war method? The answer lies in the fact that guerrilla-war provides an unfair and unreasonable advantage to a fighting force, which by traditional measure would be considered small and comparatively weak. From the times of Sun Tzu in ancient China to the communist leader Mao Zedong; from Vietnamese revolutionary forces to the Cubans – all have used guerrilla warfare to their advantage and created history. They defeated adversaries far stronger than themselves and achieved goals that looked unattainable at first. Do you think Vietnamese revolutionaries could fight the mighty French Union in a conventional war, using conventional methods? Of course not. Yet they inflicted a bitter defeat on the enemy and built the Democratic Republic of Vietnam (North Vietnam). And they did it again decades later against the powerful United States of America. Please let me say that the great Vietnamese leader Ho Chi Minh or the Great Maratha Shivaji (another champion of guerrilla warfare) were *30-something CEOs* in their own brilliant ways. They changed the rules of the game.

You might be wondering why I am discussing military tactics here in this business book, that too under a section called entrepreneurship. Consider these names –

Sachin Bansal (Co-founder, Flipkart)
Vijay Shekhar Sharma (Founder, Paytm)

Ritesh Agarwal (Founder, Oyo Rooms)

Anisha Singh (Founder, Mydala)

Shashank ND (Founder, Practo)

Kunal Bahl (Co-founder, Snapdeal)

Binny Bansal (Co-founder, Flipkart)

Deepinder Goyal (Co-founder, Zomato)

The list could go on.

Do you see what is common among all these names? They are all young Indians. They are all millionaires (some are billionaires!). They are all *30-something CEOs*, of mammoth companies. And of companies they built themselves in perhaps less than a decade. They are all entrepreneurs.

> In every success story, you will find someone who has made a courageous decision.
>
> – Peter F Drucker

And the above list is far from being exhaustive. The number of young and talented individuals in the Indian industry today who have created history by building these unicorn companies is growing with every passing day. The interesting view here is that how many of these 30-something people do you think would have become millionaire CEOs had they followed the traditional path of finding a job in someone else's company? Think about it.

They started small, they disrupted industries, they had laser-clear vision, they optimised resources and delivered results that stunned their conventional counterparts. They chose entrepreneurship over all other career options because they knew they will create more value on this path than any other. The truth is that all of them are guerrilla war leaders in modern corporate warfare.

But please understand this well and don't let these iconic names scare you. While these are the names we see on TV and the internet all the time, they are not the only extraordinary winners. There are thousands of brilliant entrepreneurs who are ordinary people like you and me, but are creating fabulous wealth for themselves and others. More importantly, they are covering a 30-year journey in a much shorter period.

At this juncture, I would like to share my own example with you.

As you might have read in the author introduction, I became the Group CEO of TBWA India at the age of 36 and led it for almost two years, before starting my new company, Talentrack. TBWA is a global top-10 advertising and communications company, and is part of the Fortune 200 Omnicom Group. Leading this supremely creative and disruptive multinational ad-agency was one of the greatest honours I have been bestowed with in my career. But the point here is, how did it happen? How did a 36-year old rise to such a significant position when most other multinational advertising CEOs in India are in their fifties or late forties at best?

It happened because I was an entrepreneur.

My first company Magnon, a full-service and exceptionally successful digital agency that I started at the age of 22, was acquired by TBWA in 2012 in its largest digital acquisition anywhere in the world. While I had over a decade's experience in leading a company which in 2012 had close to 200 employees, this acquisition gave me the opportunity to work closely with the top management of a global company. Apart from being one of the greatest learning phases of my life, that opportunity opened doors for bigger, better things, very quickly leading to my elevation to Group CEO. Now this is something I would have never got to enjoy had I been working as a regular advertising Joe for all these years. It happened only because my entrepreneurial venture catapulted me into an orbit higher than most people of my age and in my experience bracket. It happened only because I decided to be CEO of my own company at the young age of 22.

I worked extremely hard for 12 years in building a company from scratch (which I started with less than fifteen thousand rupees in my pocket), but that offered me both boundless confidence as well as the opportunity to stake claim to be CEO of a multinational company in my mid-thirties, while simultaneously creating wealth for my core team, my company and myself.

To put it more dramatically, I think I climbed the mountain.

As you might know, I have written a whole book about why and how to become an entrepreneur (titled *Build From Scratch*). It was a book I wrote when I was just 25, and had built a reasonably successful company employing close to a hundred professionals. That book sold several thousand copies and was republished by my current publisher Jaico in 2013. So that should tell you two things – one, that I can reproduce another book here on the merits of entrepreneurship; and two, that there are thousands of takers for this school of thought. You cannot, *must not* ignore it.

> As long as you are going to be thinking anyway, think big.
>
> – Donald Trump

Let's come back to the guerrilla warfare discussion, and compare it to entrepreneurship in the modern day. Of course, there is no real war going on (or is there?) in the industry, but military tactics dominate many aspects of corporate warfare even today.

So what did guerrilla warfare entail? Unconventional methods of waging war. What does entrepreneurship mean? Novel ways of creating value.

What did guerrilla warfare achieve? Unexpected gains on the enemy. What does entrepreneurship drive? Extraordinary growth as compared to peers and competitors.

What made guerrilla warfare so dreaded? It used smaller forces to inflict heavy casualties. Why is entrepreneurship so effective? It builds an organisation out of an idea.

In short, in today's fiercely competitive corporate jungle, entrepreneurship is the new guerrilla war. The names of young Indian CEOs you read above are the real Generals of contemporary times, who have defied conventional wisdom and chartered unprecedented territory – creating prosperity not just for themselves but for thousands around them.

Once again, you might think that these names are the rare few gems in the entrepreneurial world, who perhaps got lucky or had something spectacular in the form of an idea or intellect or technology that you will never have. Allow me to correct you once again, immediately and emphatically. Yes, I do agree that these are names we read about in the magazines and newspapers every now and then. But like I said before, please don't make the mistake of thinking that they are the only ones or maybe there are a handful more. There are in fact hundreds, perhaps thousands of business champions out there who may not be screaming out in the headlines of journals, but who are quietly and stylishly building large companies, creating wealth and leading as CEOs.

Every restaurant you dine in, every office you visit or every coffee shop you frequent, has an entrepreneur sitting in a corner firing away at his laptop keyboard with his bullet-like fingertips. Every hour you spend working for someone else, there is an entrepreneur pushing his cart of ideas and execution another inch towards the finish line. Once he crosses over to the other side, which he probably will, he will make in a year what most people make in a lifetime. And he will be CEO.

> "There is no passion to be found in playing small – in settling for a life that is less than what you are capable of living.
>
> \- Nelson Mandela

Like we discussed in the previous chapters, extraordinary success will come only to those who choose and dare to tread the lesser travelled road. In the industry today, it is a fact beyond debate that successful entrepreneurs grow bigger and faster than professionals in any other profile of work. If that is true, why are *you* not planning to become an entrepreneur? Of course, it is not going to be easy. Of course, there are risks involved. Sure, you will have to raise capital. Yes, it will disrupt your monthly pay check. So what? Again, so what? Believe me, you can do it. I have done it. And I say it with experience, confidence and humility – you can do it too.

People who build big companies are not superhuman. They are not even the chosen ones, and nor do they have exceptional intelligence (at least most of them don't). Successful entrepreneurs are of two kinds and pedigrees, if you ask me. The first is the real guts and glory one – With conviction, a fighter, years of slogging, sacrifice, perseverance, leading to eventual success. The second category is when everything is about perfect timing. A good idea, hospitable market sentiment, a lucky series-A investor breakthrough and a roller-coaster ride towards growth fuelled by repeated and enormous doses of investor money. Either way, determination, grit, focus and an insatiable hunger for success are common to both categories.

So if you are going to outperform everyone around you, and if you are determined bag the gold in life's race, becoming an entrepreneur is your boldest, yet surest way to success – even with all the risks involved. After all, there has never been a story of triump without risks, in the history of mankind. I can go on, but this discussion will become far too vast for the scope of this book. In my book, *Build From Scratch*, over 240 pages have been dedicated to the art and science of entrepreneurship. The book also cautions and advices those who should avoid the entrepreneurial route for reasons of age, economic security, family compulsions, and so on. At the risk of making it sound like a sales pitch, I'd like to say that *Build From Scratch* will give you all the ammunition and knowledge required to start your entrepreneurial journey.

Remember, if you want to circumvent the long queue leading to the winner's seat, you have to climb the mountain. You have to cross the desert.

Can't launch a start-up or a small company? Work for one!

> I am not a product of my circumstances. I am a product of my decisions.
>
> – Stephen Covey

No matter how much we discuss the benefits and opportunities in entrepreneurship, we need to understand and appreciate that despite all the merits of this career-choice, there will always be a section of people who are not comfortable with it. There is nothing wrong with that. Moreover, it is important to mention here that not everyone is fundamentally cut-out to start and run a business. It takes a very unique combination of temperament, ambition, risk-appetite and self-belief to become an entrepreneur. So, if after all kinds of evaluation, you still feel you don't want to take that route, please don't. Being an entrepreneur is not the only way to achieve spectacular success.

So what else can be done to break free from the mundane grind of ordinary corporate careers and reach dizzying heights of success in a comparatively short span of time? The answer is related to entrepreneurship, but without the direct risks and neck-deep commitment involved. The answer lies in working for entrepreneurial set-ups or for young, growing companies.

Let me elucidate. Like Robert Kiyosaki explains beautifully in his books, many of us have been brought-up in middle-class family set ups, where the most logical and accepted approach towards our careers, is to step out of college education and look for jobs in large, stable, and well-known companies. There is nothing much here to debate over. Big and established companies offer stability and security that we all have been hard-wired to search for. As much as I have observed amongst most Asian families, we have been tuned in to seek safety and predictability. I have not seen many families the parents or relatives encourage anyone to take up a slightly unconventional career path. All conversations are more or less about how quickly and surely we can get into a job that pays the rent, that allows us to buy a small car in two years and take a home-loan in five. How very exciting!

Again, there is nothing fundamentally wrong with looking for employment with big corporations. There is a fixed monthly income, there are healthcare benefits, retirement benefits, fixed annual holidays and more. It is an intelligent career choice. An intelligent career choice for someone who can be happy with a slow and steady professional life, and can accept that he has a one-in-a-thousand chances to make it big… really big. So you could join banks, FMCG companies, government organisations or just about any mammoth corporation. But I do hope you appreciate that this is not the route to take when you are looking at achieving in five years, what most people achieve in twenty-five.

On the other hand, let's analyse my suggestion on working for start-ups or small companies. I know some of you might take career-decisions based on what you read in this book (I do get hundreds of emails and messages from my readers, which makes me very conscious of the responsibilities involved in being a life-coach), and so, I will be brutally honest and will keep the frills and niceties at bay.

I will start with the more practical and grounded points in favour of this topic of discussion.

To begin with, in a start-up or a small company, you will have the *benefit of a superior designation.* I kid you not, even if you are just starting out, you will be able to negotiate a designation of an assistant manager or a manager with comparative ease. Young companies don't care much for organisational structures and hierarchies, which makes them nimble and adaptable. They will be happy to employ you with a fancy designation on your business card as long you fit their requirement, and you are affordable for their mostly-tight-remuneration budgets. Of course, an accelerated designation may not make a big difference to your life immediately, but it plays a huge role in crafting your resume for the future. So as long as it is not a title unreasonable to the levels of being comic, a senior designation always works in your favour. In the future, you can apply for top-tier jobs simply because you boast of a strong profile in your current employment. It will not work in isolation of course, and you will have to carry the learnings of a senior position with you, but it will definitely open up lucrative doors for you. Even if you don't see a step-up in your next company, you will at least be able to get hired at title of the same level – from being senior manager in a small start-up, you will probably jump to being senior manager in a larger company. This is speeding you up by at least four or five years.

The second thing you will benefit immensely from when you join a small company is *a participative, and sometimes – submissive boss*. I know this is rather harsh, but most entrepreneurs in their early years are heavily dependent on their team. Deep down, they know they need you more than you need them. While this equation does not last for too long and gets duly reversed as the company starts becoming successful, this early stage can help you extract a lot of benefits from your employer. These can be in the form of monetary benefits, designation (as discussed above), role, working hours, reporting structure, industry opportunities and more. Since the number of people willing to join start-ups and new ventures is far lower than the workforce available to large companies, your employer will value you significantly more than what you will be valued as in a big company. This will lead to faster salary hikes, promotions, leadership opportunities, market exposure, client relationships, etc., to name a few. Last but not the least – you will appreciate this point more if you are already working – you will get to work for someone who treats you more like a partner than an employee. And that is priceless.

> Great things are done by a series of small things brought together.
>
> \- Vincent Van Gogh

Let me now come to the softer but equally important advantages that come with working for a young company.

The third clear plus point of joining a small company is *the work-content that will come your way* very early in your career. The good thing about entrepreneurial set-ups is that everyone does everything. Roles are not defined in water-tight compartments and everyone gets to contribute in a variety of ways. So, not only do you get to learn about the work areas that you are directly responsible for, but you also get exposed to a rich spectrum of other organisational aspects. This obviously makes your learning curve steep and offers you an insight into running a company at a very comprehensive level. This learning will equip you for bigger and better leadership roles in the future and will shape you into an exceptionally capable professional.

Let me explain the above third benefit with an example. I hired Vivek Merani, my colleague now at Magnon, and also one of my closest friends and trusted confidantes, when he was just 20. At that time, I was all of 22. This was the time I started my first company with a shoestring budget. Like they say in *amchi* Mumbai: *boley toh chillad ke vaande they*! I picked him during his college education and that too at quite a paltry pay package. That was all I could afford at that time and Vivek was the best person I could spot in my immediate circle to play the role of my employee cum partner. So anyone looking at the situation then might have felt that it was not so much of a great deal for Vivek, and not so much of a high-quality partner for me. Well, that's how the start-up world works – on compromises and on making the best use of what you have. However, the same observer would today look at Vivek and me, and say that this was the best deal either of us could have got. I got the best partner I could have asked for, and Vivek got to rise very quickly in life. His growth was aligned with the company's growth curve at every step. He got the best of designations, the fastest wage-hikes, the maximum exposure and unquestioned respect. Today at 35, he is a 30-something CEO himself, leading our international digital/production company Magnon eg+ as Managing Director. Although Vivek is exceptionally talented, I don't see how he would have become MD of a multinational agency at such a young age, had he chosen any other conventional career-path.

The last but equally important advantage of working with a start-up is *the hard & result-oriented business training that it provides.* Let's face it. Most start-ups (except those that are funded with unreasonable burn-money available) spend every waking hour fighting for survival. They need every dollar they can earn to stay afloat. While this does make things a bit challenging for everyone in the team, it imparts priceless education at a sub-conscious level. It makes you understand the importance of revenue. It teaches you how to make every day count. It makes you aware of how costs are monitored. It shows you how a team comes together in the harshest of circumstances. It allows you to observe a leader who never loses hope, who is never short of energy and who keeps on fighting relentlessly. These lessons make you a very hardened professional, yet with a softness that only a start-up employee can have. It gives you the determination to deliver results no matter what happens, and it allows you to feel a sense of belongingness to the organisation. And a goal-oriented person who feels for the company is precisely what every employer is looking for.

> "Whenever you find yourself on the side of the majority, it is time to pause and reflect.
>
> – Mark Twain

I am sure by now you have a good understanding of how working with a start-up can be a close alternative to running one yourself. Like I have repeated several times by now, you will have to choose a path that looks difficult at the beginning, appears different from what the others are doing, but has the maximum return-on-investment in terms of your career growth. Today, some of the fastest-rising super-achievers across the world are people who are entrepreneurs or those who have had a close association with one. You will seldom find a glossy business magazine story of someone young with a boring banking career (unless he turns out to be a best-selling fiction author!) or someone who worked with a large automobile company. You will mostly read about people who took novel routes to create value for themselves and for the society.

Start thinking actively about both the above acceleration methods that we have analysed. If you want to start a company, do it now. There is never a better time. If you want to enter the world of start-ups as an employee, go for it. They are waiting for you!

> The speed of the boss is the speed of the team.
>
> – Lee Iacocca

building your corporate 'militia'

Why 'generals' have been the greatest assets of conquerors over centuries; and how nothing has changed

They hunt in packs. They live and fight together. Operating like one large unified organism, they defeat adversaries far stronger than them. They win in the harshest of circumstances and they give each other strength. Their survival instinct is seconded only by their desire to watch each other's backs. They question each other when alone, but scream their battle-cry in unison when out there in the field. Their tale travels far. They are respected and feared by friends and enemies alike. They know their individual glory is upheld by the sweat and blood of the brotherhood. They have witnessed victories that came only because they fought rubbing shoulders with one other. I am talking about modern-day business warfare. And about the corporate warlords and *militias* that rule it even today. Nothing has changed.

You might be wondering what exactly I am talking about. What relevance does a *militia* have in today's industry parlance? Which warlords am I referring to? Who are these people who hunt in packs and work like one cohesive force? What brotherhood? I know. It is hard to fathom what I am saying in the first shot. This is because it is a very rare phenomenon. A phenomenon that paves way for corporate fairy-tales. An occurrence that takes a legendary leader and very special followers coming together. A game-changer.

What is a corporate 'militia'?

Every time you read the story of a great victor in history, you will discover, on scratching the surface, that he was surrounded by a battery of loyal and incorruptible lieutenants. Akbar, the Great had his *navratnas* or nine gems. King Arthur had his forty knights around his fabled round table. Japanese emperors ruled under the able protection of the Samurai and even Jesus had His apostles.

Now take a close look at today's business maharajas. Narayana Murthy from Infosys started the company with seven co-founders (including Nandan Nilekani and Kris Gopalakrishnan). Dhirubhai Ambani was known to have a close coterie of confidantes who assisted him in running the massive Reliance empire. Even young entrepreneurs today, fresh out of their engineering colleges, are forming teams of six to ten before approaching venture capital firms with their start-up ideas. In short, although we see the name and face of one key promoter behind most success stories, it is really a team of loyalists that sticks together through thick and thin to make winning possible. This team is nothing but a modern-day corporate militia. Or so I would like to call it.

Let me to explain this concept in detail. As we all know, there are no substitutes for hard-work and team-work. Now imagine the two coming together, and that too, for years at length. Imagine a hard-working team committed to a cause on a long-term basis. Think about all that can be achieved when smart and capable people team up together, and share a collective dream. When they work towards a common goal relentlessly, under the stewardship of a visionary leader. Wait a minute...wasn't this happening when Alexander the Great embarked upon his imperial journey? Wasn't this collective dream the driving force behind Subhash Chandra Bose and the Indian National Army? While I don't mean to compare cold business with the noble cause of Netaji, we cannot ignore the similarities between the evolution of great leaders in history and the building of organisations in modern times. Both have one critical success factor backing them – a team of bold and devoted people - a militia.

> Talent wins games, but teamwork and intelligence win championships.
>
> – Michael Jordan

What is the relevance of a militia or a devoted team to a discussion about your journey towards becoming a *30-something CEO*? And even if it is important and relevant on a larger level, how is it of any use to you in particular? You don't have a devoted set of followers, and why should you? You're not a leader or a corporate statesman. Why do you need to get into this discussion?

Let me tell you why – because you will need to be a leader or corporate statesman to arrive at the goals we are talking about. No journey towards success is possible if you travel alone. One of the greatest mistakes mediocre people make is that they believe that their career is dependent only on them. What they miss out is that a true winner never views himself in isolation. He understands very early in his career that he will need a circle of friends, a parallel family that he gets to choose, to assist and protect him at every step. The corporate sector is not very different from the corridors of political power. It has its own share of politicking, planning, manoeuvring and gamesmanship. Sometimes the battles are fought behind the veils of smiling faces and crisp suits.

While at times, they are fought like pitched battles, openly and brazenly. In both these forms of business warfare, you will need comrades and partners who can fight by your side. I will explain this in greater detail as we progress further into this chapter.

Like I said earlier, even the greatest conquerors and business tycoons need their trusted team. So if you are going for the kill and be a *30-something CEO*, you will need to build that team as well. I will first tell you what that team will do for you and then describe how you can start working right away towards building one.

From Sherwood Forest to Gurgaon and Bandra-Kurla – The Hood & His Merry Men

One of the most exciting stories I read as a child was that of the Prince of Thieves, Robin Hood - the archer, the warrior, the beloved of the poor, the nightmare of the tyrants, the charming lover and the witty swordsman. The one thing I will never forget about his stories and adventures is his inseparable band of merry men – Robin's band of friends and followers in Lincoln green clothes, travelling, fighting and living in the forests of Sherwood together. Whether it was Little John or Friar Tuck or Alan A'dale, the legend of Robin of Locksley will never be complete without the stories of his partners riding alongside him. Or should we say, there might have never been a legend at all, had Robin not nurtured and enjoyed the camaraderie of this jolly and valiant team.

There is a great lesson to be learnt from the mystical character of Robin Hood. Apart from the ease with which he would sell stolen meat in exchange for kisses from pretty lasses of course, there are enormous management lessons in his life and adventures. The greatest among them being his natural gift for team-building and retention! As you read the stories of how each of his merry men joined his band, you will observe a common trend. Robin was quick to spot talent. Even quicker was he in offering his hand of friendship. This team-building and nurturing is something we will examine at length in the next section on how you can build your own band in today's organisations. What is important to note here is the help Robin gets from his band of brothers at every stage of his adventurous life. Whether it was his bold daylight rescue attempt, his combats with stronger adversaries or even the last few moments of his life, Robin Hood was always protected by his men and vice versa. No wonder they are legends today, and their names are taken together in the same breath.

Now compare this to the situations you might have to face during your arduous climb (and arduous it will be!) to the peak of success. We have discussed this earlier – that you will not reach the dizzying heights of extraordinary success by waiting for that promotion every five years. You will have to hustle, be nimble and enterprising, move in uncharted territories and find footholds where others can't. It goes without saying, that this speed and planned aggression will make you an enemy to many and you will have to stay ready to face fierce personal and professional onslaughts.

> "Tom, don't let anybody kid you. It's all personal, every bit of business."
>
> – The Godfather

Let me explain it to you with my own example. Once, I got into a major organisational battle with the CEO of a leading group agency. It was a turf war. He wanted to overpower me and get my agencies under his leadership. I wanted the same and wanted his agency to fall under my management. He had seniority on his side (being ten years older than me) and was well entrenched into the system. He was also an advertising veteran and was exceptionally smart. On the other hand, I was a significant shareholder in my company and my business was far more profitable than his. It was anybody's game.

The one factor that tilted the scales in my favour was the loyalty of my core leadership team. Over 17 years of being in the industry I have succeeded in building a strong team (*militia!*) of very capable professionals who work with me like family. The battle between this CEO and me raged on for over a year, and went through several cycles of ups and downs. We were both experienced gamers and took it all as part of the deal. The difference however soon started showing. My team and I worked like a single organism, converting every turn of events into our advantage. I had deep conviction that while my adversary was a seasoned professional, I was a superior leader in terms of people, vision and result-orientation. Thankfully, my team shared this conviction and wanted to see me emerge as the leader. It was soon evident to the worldwide leadership of our corporation that I enjoyed the unquestioned support of my senior team (still do!) whereas my competitor could not boast of any such allegiance from his colleagues. I won the battle.

It is vital to grasp the importance of having a protective shield of capable individuals around you. It is certainly not a one-sided affair. You give them as much support as they give you. That is how it works best. That is how it is sustainable.

Let me give another example of how this approach works well for everyone. A senior leader I know in the industry, has developed a group of confidantes around him. There was a time when he used to report to me, and from what I know of him and have observed, he is not a very good businessperson at an individual level. But he is a popular guy. His group of people consists of all tiers of seniority. He has a deep bond with someone quite close to his own stature, but also has a few youngsters who look up to him and consider him their mentor. He moves jobs every four to five years, and within a year of his move, his entire coterie follows him! This gives them all an opportunity to flourish together, and most of all, it helps him create a secure and familiar environment around him wherever he goes.

The cool part about this whole strategy is that it drives collective welfare and safety for everyone in the brotherhood. The seniors benefit from the undying loyalty of a solid team, whereas the team gets a permanent mentor and guide. The added advantage is that sooner or later, the organisation, and then the industry, becomes aware of this band. This awareness leads to a lot of people trying to join in, and also to a certain awe with which people start viewing this group and its members. However, in most cases such units are not really visible to the common eye. They keep it under wraps and operate like a covert outfit. Or sometimes a strong group exists but not in the immediate consciousness of the members. They know they have friends but fail to notice how they can work together towards shared goals. Whatever the case may be, the brotherhood (or sisterhood) is more effective than any one individual can be.

Many of you may be wondering what I am talking about. I know this concept is tough to fully understand and to identify with. That is because it is a rare phenomenon like I said right at the beginning. Most successful entrepreneurs are champions at building these solid crews and you will see almost all of them have this human firewall of dependable people around them. Most rapidly successful corporate leaders are also masters of this art. But it is not something you will notice unless you look for it. It works all around you, but only when you pause to take cognizance does it unveil itself.

> Watch with glittering eyes the whole world around you because the greatest secrets are always hidden in the most unlikely places. Those who don't believe in magic will never find it.
>
> \- Roald Dahl

The crazy part is that a lot of people are unable to see this force even when they are standing at its doorstep. Not everyone understands these strategic modus operandi. I have seen people who reject this idea as some kind of sycophancy or subservience to the leader. In my opinion, it is nothing but false ego that holds one back from growth. They fail to see that there is absolutely no sycophancy when everyone knows it is a symbiotic arrangement. The leader of the bunch benefits only as much as the rest of the members, and has to retain his position and the unity of the group by making sure that the collective and mutual advantage is never lost.

Leading such a group or being part of one will serve you in many ways. It offers security of your current job. This is because you have a group of people around you who talk favourably about you and watch out for you. People who work in multinational companies or large domestic organisations will appreciate what I am saying. They would perhaps recognize how large companies or organisations become hot beds of corporate politics and how important it is to safeguard one's interests. Being part of a close-knit team insulates you from bumps on the road and every offensive move from your competitors. It also offers you significant leverage with the management of the organisation simply because no one likes to fire someone who is popular and who influences opinions.

There are many other advantages that your *militia* will bring with it. You will never be short of references and will have opportunities opening themselves whenever your teammates move. You will always have a trusted group of friends to choose from in case you need to hire someone in or around your team. If you choose to take the entrepreneurial route, anytime in the future, you know where to find able and loyal co-founders. The list could go on.

To encapsulate what I have said so far – please remember that your career depends as much on the people around you as it depends on your own effort. Don't make the mistake of thinking that only people senior to you in stature can help you. You will be amazed to observe the impact that your juniors have on your career progression. Build your own corporate *militia* my friend, starting now.

I hear you asking *'But how'*?

Find the Warlord in you – How to build your own business-militia

We discussed in the previous section how much help Robin Hood would have got from his merry men, and how the modern-day Robin Hood is no different. We, however, did not decode the methods by which such a band could be built. Clearly, it is not an easy task – which is why, solid teams are hard to find.

There are many reasons why such *militias* are rare. First and foremost, it is difficult to spot like-minded people who can stick together for years – not necessarily being in the same organisation (though preferably so), as long as they work like a cohesive unit. But in a world full of insecurities, egos and competitiveness, finding such camaraderie is indeed tough. Moreover, not everyone is as career-focused as you are (since you have picked-up this book to read, I am assuming you have the hunger in you to become a *30-something CEO*). So not everyone will value such a group. Most importantly, since most people would not have seen such a crew in action over the years, it will be hard to find common ground.

Yet, leaders do it. They find the right people. They fit them into the right roles. They build relationships of deep trust. They retain such people and nurture this *militia* over years. Painstakingly, but surely. Remember none of them are born leaders. They have learnt this art as they have grown. If they can, so can you.

> We're all working together; that's the secret.
>
> **- Sam Walton**

Now let me highlight a few ways in which this goal can be achieved. All of these may not work for you, but I am sure you will find a connect somewhere which will help you start this project today. Take a look at the below points:

1. **Sense of Purpose** – The foremost factor towards building your core group will be your own determination to do it. I started myself on this path 17 years ago. I am still working on it because I know this is a continuous journey. Today, my *militia* has nine

Generals – each more capable than the other. Even so, I still do not rest. I am extremely selective about who I welcome into this core group and I am still on the lookout for more partners. So you have to be absolutely committed to this cause. People will betray your trust, as many have betrayed mine over the years. But that is part of the game. For every successful General you succeed in bringing into the *militia*, you will have to work on three at the very least. In other words, if you aim to have, say four trusted partners over the next five years, you will need to shortlist at least twelve and work towards winning their trust and friendship. How you will do that will be covered in the points to come. But remember – you will succeed in building your *militia* only if you are determined to do so.

2. **Honesty & Transparency** – You will not succeed in this objective if you approach it with an intent of using people. It doesn't work that way. There will have to be genuine respect and affection between you and your band members. There is not a single person in my own core *militia* whom I don't love deeply. I admit it wasn't this way when we started, but the love has grown over the years as we have fought several battles together, side by side. Even at the outset, I have always only welcomed people I felt very positive about. Today I can safely say that they are not only my

trusted colleagues, not only my best friends, but also members of my family. I am certain it is the same with them. We have lasted all these years (touchwood) only because we have been honest and transparent with each other. We know we are a corporate-*militia* and each one of us knows that I have built it purposefully. We all believe that we have seen our successes because we are together. We talk about it openly and fondly. Do keep this in mind while building your core crew. Let them know what you are planning. Talk to them about how important they are to you and how much value you want to add to their lives. This is the only way to win their trust and friendship in the long run.

3. **Remember – it's symbiosis** – Even with all the right intentions and all the sincerity in place, it is important to know that this is a give and take arrangement after all. There is nothing wrong with that. Be aware of what you bring to the table and what you expect in return. What I offer to my teammates is one hundred percent job security (as they all work in my companies), highest levels of respect, protection from external forces that might harm them, rapid career growth and prosperity. What I ask in return is unquestioned loyalty and continuity. It works well for all of us. Now you may or may not have the advantage of having all of your team members working for you. So you will need to ensure that they see value in being

your comrade. You could be a great networker, you could be someone who can open doors for them, your expertise or knowledge may be of great use to them, or you could simply be someone they can rely on for anything and everything. You will be pleasantly surprised to see how many people value the last trait immensely. Whatever it is that you offer, you should be aware of it and you should continuously chip away at bettering it.

4. **Find the Warlord in you** – Since we are generously using the term *militia* to describe these informal yet highly-effective corporate brotherhoods, there is no harm in using the title, *Warlord*, for their leaders. Quite frankly these guys are warlords of sorts, leading men and women, protecting their turfs and winning more corporate territory. I truly believe we all have a warlord or a leader hidden within each of us. Some people find the warlord within faster than the others. It comes to some of us more naturally than it comes to the others. But all of us have one within us for sure. While we may all not have the gift or charisma of a great leader to begin with, we can most definitely develop this quality as the years progress. There are thousands of books written on this topic, and so I will not address it in too much detail. Just remember Robin Hood once again. Did you know he was at first beaten in one-to-one battles by almost all his key

confidantes? Yet, he hired them and led them as their natural leader.

5. **For God's sake… Socialise!** – What do you think was the genesis of the phrase *'breaking bread together'*? Are you aware that the Indian Air Force even today has the culture of a *'badaa khaana'* where the officers and the men dine together? Did you know that it is a custom among certain Arab countries to have members of a family eat from the same plate? Would you know why all this is done? A lot of people think that offices close with the close of business hours. They miss a very crucial point here. Yes, it does wrap-up business for the day for a majority of the people working there. However, the real networking, bonding and gameplay often happens post office hours or even during weekends. At the end of the day (literally) we are dealing with human beings. The more informal time we spend together the more closeness we tend to build. I feel sorry for people who pick-up their bags and head home as soon as office hours are over. They often don't realise how much action they miss out on. I am certainly not saying one should eat into one's family time for this kind of networking, but an evening out with a few beers or a having hot meal along with office colleagues, seniors and friends, once in a couple of weeks, is not so much of an ask. The return on investment is immense. We will talk about

this again in the last chapter, where we will deep-dive into some essential traits of a *30-something CEO*.

> Alone we can do so little. Together we can do so much.
>
> \- Helen Keller

Before we close this discussion, I must once again say that I have put in a lot of thinking in writing this chapter. This is a seldom talked about concept and is not really visible on the surface. It takes us into some darker but practical aspects of today's competitive organisations. It forces us to admit that politics, conspiracy and gamesmanship are rife in modern-day organisations and industry. But I felt compelled to share this knowledge with you. This *militia* and core group strategy has worked wonders for me, as it has for perhaps hundreds and thousands of leaders over the history of mankind. I am sure it will work for you as well, as you climb the steep mountain of success, equipped with nothing but your burning desire to win.

> Let us rather run the risk of wearing out than rusting out.
>
> – Theodore Roosevelt

"dad, why do fighter-pilots become commanding officers?"

The P&L riders; and the pencil-pushers

One of the things I am very proud of is that I hail from an Indian Air Force officer's family. My dearest father Gp Capt (Retd) DN Bajpai retired from the Air Force over a decade ago. We remember the days of our lives in Air Force stations with great affection and nostalgia. Living in close vicinity of the forces for around two decades, I also got the opportunity to observe them very closely and admire the systems and discipline they follow. As would be expected, we did not understand every nuance very clearly and had to ask dad for clarifications.

One such trend I noticed was that the station commanders were mostly pilots, majority of them being fighter-pilots. The Indian Air Force is an equal opportunity employer and looks after the welfare and career growth of its people like few other world-class organisations. To get a basic understanding, you need to know that not everyone in the Air Force flies aeroplanes. There are what are called 'Ground Duties' as well, which include engineers, air traffic control (ATC), meteorology, admin and more. These officers and men are as critical to the efficient functioning of the force as the pilots are. Without their support no pilot would agree to take-off with his jet fighter.

When I saw most station commanders coming from the flying side, it was very natural for me to ask my father as to why this was so. He gave me an answer that I will always remember. He simply said, "*Even though our planes and safety standards are very advanced and best-in-class, fighter-pilots risk their lives for the nation every time they take-off. They are the ones who understand the pressures of facing the enemy eye-to-eye, which equips them to lead an elite fighting force."* I was convinced immediately. The message was loud and clear. The higher the risk and pressures, higher the return in terms of organisational seniority and growth. As fair as it can get.

Now, how is this anecdote relevant to the discussion about *the 30-something CEO*? Let me explain. The example of the Indian Air Force is not unique in itself. Most organisations in the world today have a well-defined structure in terms of departments, expertise, regions, offices, teams and more. These structures evolve over time and align in a way that is most suited for the functioning of the organisation. And almost all these organisations have 'field' and 'non-field' jobs and specialisations. Some of these are considered to be more demanding than the others. This changes from industry to industry, but in all cases there are these people who stand directly in the line of fire.

Please allow me to elaborate on this further in the next section.

The line of fire

Back in 2008, we hired a young man named Nikhil (name changed), an excellent Business Development resource at our company Magnon. He was all of 28, but had immense talent for sales. As most growing companies, we had tremendous respect for our Sales and Account Management teams. We knew they were doing the heavy lifting, winning new clients and keeping the old ones happy in an extremely competitive digital media market. Nikhil was doing well month after month, quarter after quarter. In our usual participative style, we made it no secret that we admired him and his contribution to the company. He saw an out-of-turn wage-hike and was soon promoted to a managerial position, a rarity for someone his age. We spoke about him often in our management meetings and all of us in the senior team were looking forward to seeing him grow further in the company.

And then one day he called it a day. We did not see it coming as he was on a roll and we were almost sure he was enjoying every minute of it. But he wasn't. The reason for leaving, as he said, was that he couldn't handle the pressure of sales! He could not get himself to wake-up every morning staring at a revenue target that he had to achieve. I spent a long time with him, explaining to him that the ability to handle this pressure of expectations and numbers is what makes the most precious and sought-after professionals in the industry. I reminded him of how he rose to a manager's position so swiftly and how he won a pay-raise in a very short span of time. During our discussion, I assured him of a stellar career with us if he continued to perform the way he had been performing so far. I gave him numerous examples of how it was the sales people who rose the fastest and highest in companies, because they faced the heat and got in the money. Nevertheless, an hour into the conversation I realised he had shut himself to any advice and was stubbornly insisting on leaving.

After a while I gave up and asked him what he was going to do. He told me he was going to move to a mid-sized company and join as an internal operations manager. I could not believe my ears as I knew he had an exceptional flair for client-facing areas of business and he would not hit his true potential in an internal op profile. But he was adamant and he left. From what I hear of him, so many years later, his career hasn't really taken-off and he is among the thousands of mediocre managers in the industry today. He could have been a star. He could have been a *30-something CEO*.

Nikhil is not the only example of how very capable people often lose track simply because they want to escape the pressures of measurable performances. Allow me to explain why I add the word 'measurable' before performance. We know that all winning organisations in the world function with a deep performance culture. Meritocracy is the order of the day and evaluation is done on very objective parameters. So, a sales professional can be evaluated very accurately simply because her contribution can be measured in terms of clear numbers – revenue, order-booking, repeat business or whatever the business' metrics are. There is no ambiguity whatsoever. Similarly, a software engineer can be assessed with great precision based on the quantity and quality of the code he writes, or the number of modules he delivers in a stipulated time-frame. Again, there are many verticals in businesses where people can be evaluated with ease and clarity. And not everyone likes that.

Then there are some departments or areas in every company that are not so easy to control, monitor and assess, although most business organisations today like to have evaluation systems in place that cover everyone right from the CEO to the security personnel. Internal rewards and recognition programmes have been receiving a lot of attention in modern organisations, as it has now been proven beyond doubt that people are the differentiating factor in a company's long-term success and failure. Thus, measurement of performance is a priority today, for large corporations and small businesses alike. However, there are still some limitations that introduce subjectivity and fuzziness into performance assessment in some areas of business. And some people like that.

Before I move any further, it is important that I emphatically underline my boundless respect for every specialisation in the corporate sector and in the business community at large. I have led a company(s) for over 17 years now and I understand as well as anybody else, that an organisation flourishes only when it sees balanced growth and performance across all its departments. Philip Kotler elucidated in the very first chapter of one of his fantastic books on how marketing and customer orientation of the entire organisation is important for the success of a company. So whether it is production, marketing, sales, human resources, operations, information technology, supply chain, front desk, customer support, legal, procurement or any other department, each plays an equally critical role in the functioning of an organisation. Quite like the Air Force example I took earlier, where the pilots and the ground duty teams work shoulder to shoulder.

However, it would be incorrect and unfair to say that all specialisations have the same risk and return curve. Again, just like in the Air Force example, all businesses have and need their own 'fighter pilots'. These are people who contribute to the hardest yet most critical ends of the business. And since they work at the most critical ends of the business, the evaluation and measurement of performance are at their highest levels. But so are the rewards and returns. And you will notice that most people who rise exceptionally fast in their careers, hail from these high-risk, high-return specialisations.

> "You were born to win, but to be a winner you must plan to win, prepare to win, and expect to win.
>
> - Zig Ziglar

Those of us with some experience in the industry would have observed that in most cases the turn-around in sales teams are mostly higher than what you will probably see in human resources. However, we would have also noticed that the pay-packets of people in sales and their incentives/promotions are far more lucrative than most other departments. You may have also witnessed that most people in the corner offices are from these 'life-blood' departments that keep the revenue and profitability of the company going. Since they have the magnifying glass of the top management over them at all times, their life becomes more difficult than those in departments that work quietly for months or even years without being monitored directly or even indirectly by the big bosses. So, here is what happens – the guys who don't perform well get red-flagged very quickly and may be asked to leave the department or the company. As simple as that. Those who do perform become the darlings of the senior management, and slowly but surely, become indispensable. The leadership starts going out of its way to keep such people close and happy. They give anything and everything to these invaluable people – respect, money, designations, opportunities and much more. Thus, begins the rise of *the 30-something CEO.*

The dynamics are very clear. Those who do the heavy-lifting get the fattest pay cheques and the fastest growth tracks. The problem arises when many of us hope to get that fat pay cheque without being willing to do the heavy-lifting.

Just like in the example I have given above about Nikhil, many of us try to stay away from high-pressure roles. We do not realise that those roles are high-pressured because they are important! People who take such jobs and deliver, will always be more valuable to an organisation than people looking for safer jobs. You see, everyone can do a safe job! If you think you can identify a cushy position and the management of the company cannot, you're wrong. Everyone knows what jobs are easy and which ones are tough. There is always a premium attached to the tougher roles. In fact, the tougher the job, more the premium. One of the key things you need to understand while drawing the blueprint of your career, is that you cannot avoid risk and hard-work, while you still hope to be a super-successful individual. There is no such convenient short-cut available.

There is no easy way out.

Riding with the warriors

So before we move ahead, let us agree on one important point. When you are galloping towards the goal of becoming a *30-something CEO*, you cannot be on the lookout for comfort, be it mental or physical. You cannot hope to have an easy 9 to 5 job that also gives you ample time to indulge in office gossip, update your Facebook status a few times and go on for long lunch-breaks. The journey towards magnificent success is penance. It needs ambition, discipline, enterprise, creativity – but most of all, it demands back-breaking effort from you.

> The woods are lovely, dark and deep. But I have promises to keep. And miles to go before I sleep, And miles to go before I sleep.
>
> – Robert Frost

I like to compare ambitious young business executives of today with warriors of the olden times. Aren't markets the new battlefields, companies the new kingdoms and CEOs the new emperors? What I suggest to you is that you transform yourself into a modern-day warrior. That you choose to ride with the other fighters in the boldest of battlefields, rather than rust away in the oblivion of commoners. Ride with the other *30-something CEOs*.

What I am simply asking you to do is to identify the high-octane, high-growth opportunities available to you. Forget about what roles or jobs fall within your comfort zone. Break free and search for the most challenging yet rewarding prospects you can find. Wherever you are now and whatever work you do, or if you are a student preparing to get into the corporate arena, try and align yourself into the very mainstream of your organisation. You will never be able to gather the speed of a mainline player if you continue working in the sidelines. It would be different for different companies, industries and even markets. So, let's try and see how we can spot the juicy yet thorny end of the business – so we can go after it full-steam, fearlessly, with absolute belief that we can do it.

At this point, I would like to share another slice of my own experience with you. I am doing this because I feel at numerous points in my life, I identified opportunities that I felt were lucrative and went after them irrespective of whether I had the requisite skillset or not. It may sound silly but as you read on you might see sense in it. Most importantly, I am not trying to blow my own trumpet. I have innumerable shortcomings and weaknesses like all human beings. Just that I truly feel I may be able to drive home a vital point here.

> The successful warrior is the average man, with laser-like focus.
>
> – Bruce Lee

When I was working in GE Capital, I witnessed the great dotcom surge and discussed with my friends and superiors, my plans to start my very own digital agency. They thought I was mad. I was all of 22, had no money, no experience in digital media and could not answer all the hard questions they asked me. But then, this exercise made me even more determined to go after my dream and I started a tiny company despite everyone's cautions and warnings. That company today is Magnon – one of Asia's largest digital agencies.

In 2001, when I was a year into running my own company, I was short of cash. Most entrepreneurs are. Sometimes, I did not even have enough to fuel up my motorcycle. This made me think of options like teaching at management institutions in order to use the extra income for my upkeep, while my company would grow and I could continue reinvesting every penny into it. Once again, people raised eyebrows when I shared my thoughts with them. They reminded me that I was only 23 (perhaps younger than most students I was planning to teach), did not have a B.Ed. or PhD (I did have a MBA though), and clearly no teaching experience. Within two weeks of my first thought, I was teaching a class full of MBA students at a reputed B-school. I met the director and was able to convince him that I could teach. Being very young, wearing earrings to class worked to my advantage. Soon, I became the favourite among my students. Since then, I have taught thousands of management graduates, some of whom are very well-placed in the industry today.

One day, while reading a business book, I felt I could write one too. I was 25 then, and had succeeded in getting a small company to its feet within three short years. I was making a bit of money, and so I thought I should share my experience of starting a business ground-up through a book. As always, there were wry smiles from friends and family when I told them about it. Everyone thought it was a crazy idea that would die its own death gradually. A year and a half later, my first business book, *Build From Scratch* was released by a Union Minister at a glittering event in New Delhi. It sold thousands of copies and is even now considered a must-read for budding entrepreneurs.

When I was 35, I expressed my desire to lead a multinational advertising agency to the worldwide leadership of our corporation. My close advisors were worried because I had zero experience in hard-core advertising. While I had successfully led a large digital agency for many years and was well-versed with the management of an agency, pure-play advertising was a different ball-game. Yet, I knew this step was crucial for the next phase of my career and I pressed on. I took over as CEO of the agency in March 2014 and within 12 months we were able to deliver a financial year that was better than any of the previous years in a decade, and improved its industry ranking by seven positions as per a leading advertising magazine.

My decision to launch my new company, Talentrack, was again something that a lot of people around me could not understand. I was leading one of the most reputed advertising groups in India, was on an enviable pay package and at 37, I was living the dream that most people in the industry cherish. Yet, during late 2015, I stepped down from that position to launch Talentrack. This time, even my Dad was flabbergasted! He asked me why I was after so much fame, money, and comfort. I was disrupting my life and embarking upon an entrepreneurial journey yet again. He actually used the phrase '*punishing yourself*'! He was right in many ways, but the truth is that I believe my journey was not meant to stop at being a CEO. There was so much more to do. I have deep conviction that Talentrack is going to change the talent-hiring and networking dynamics of the mammoth media, entertainment, creative & art (MECA) industries, and in the process will generate spectacular value for its promoters, investors, employees, partners and other stakeholders. Perhaps already the largest talent-platform for the MECA industries in India, it will empower artists and make this world a better place for millions of them.

The reason why I have described the episodes from my life is to point out that you have to spot opportunities for yourself and not wait for them to fall into your lap. I am a regular guy like any of us, but sometimes you have to actually create opportunities like I did when I started Talentrack. Or when I chose to write that book. No one asked me to do it. It was not something anyone would have missed in my profile. Yet, that book gave me fame and credibility that is unparalleled. It made me get worldwide recognition as a business writer and got me featured in global media. I *chose* that extra bit of work. Trust me it is not easy writing a book. More than the knowledge and/or experience that is required, it is the perseverance and solitude that are most demanding. The book you are holding in your hands is my third book. I did not need to write it given the punishing work schedule I have. But I chose to. As I write these words I am sitting alone in my study on a late Saturday evening when all my friends are out clubbing and fine-dining. But then, I am the only one in the circle who has over 1,00,000 followers on social media. I am the only *30-something CEO.*

> If somebody offers you an amazing opportunity but you are not sure you can do it, say yes – then learn how to do it later.
>
> **- Richard Branson**

My appeal to you would be that you don't run away from hard-work. Don't shy-away from real pressure. Instead, look for it. Embrace it! Look at it as an ally rather than a threat. Give yourself more challenges. Aim for bigger things. Push your boundaries and stun yourself and others with an undying commitment towards winning. It is better to come back home and crumble into deep sleep as a result of the sweet fatigue of intense hard-work, than to be home early only to watch more TV and to watch more people whiz past you on the road to triumph.

The Arena

You will not believe how fed-up I am of meeting people who ask for career advice but walk into my office and exclaim, *"I don't want to do sales!"*. Well, this world runs on sales. You bought this book because there was a salesman trying to sell it. You may or may not have seen him, but believe me he was there somewhere in the background when you were buying this book online. Before this book was published, I had to sell myself and the concept to my publisher. If Amish Tripathi or Chetan Bhagat sell millions of copies of their books, it is because apart from their writing excellence there is also an enormous sales and marketing machinery behind the success of their titles. Our beloved Prime Minister Narendra Modi is travelling the world asking developed countries to come and 'Make in India'. He is *selling* the India story to the globe. When a start-up goes out to raise funds, the promoters *sell* the idea to venture capital firms. Like I said, our whole ecosystem thrives on sales! Capable and goal-oriented sales people are an asset to any organisation. No wonder some of the most rapidly growing professionals come from this bold and stylish business stream. Yet some people want to stay away from it. Why?

> No pressure, no diamonds.
>
> – Thomas Carlyle
> (Scottish Philosopher & Writer)

Let us try and demystify this whole discussion and bring you closer to what can be done practically by each one of us to get into the real action. Please understand that I am not asking you to abandon what you are doing and jump into a completely unknown territory. Nor am I asking you to forsake the stability of your current occupation. All I am recommending is an analysis of where you are and what you do, and if we can add some value to it by checking on some meatier openings nearby... some opportunities that might push you from the slow street to the fast highway. (Okay, I loved this statement because it has the title of my second book *The Street to the Highway* in it!)

The easiest way to assess whether you are in the right stream or should be switching orbits is to ask the simple question – *Do I make a direct impact on the P&L (profit and loss) of my company?* Period. That's it. This is really the essence of it all, the name of the game. I know this sounds too much like a broad brush-stroke and sweeping statement, but believe me, it is true in most cases and companies. Your contribution could be directly reflecting on the P&L or making a significant impact on it indirectly, but you *have* to be in the P&L game. Like I said earlier, the turf changes from company to company, industry to industry. You will need to choose your work specialisation based on the dynamics of your organisation.

P&L impacting specialisations may not always be the same across industries. For example, a BPO (business process outsourcing) company that employs thousands of people and is totally dependent on manpower, will have human resources

(HR) as a mission-critical function. It will be a tough job, loads of accountability, but it is just the kind of action you need to be in the middle of, if you want to win as an HR professional. Similarly, an investment bank will look for the ability to win the trust of clients and deal-making as the most important talents. A consumer goods brand will consider its marketing & brand management teams as the most crucial departments driving the fortunes of the company. A creative designer may not be so much of a star at a law firm or a bank, but an advertising agency will treat him as premium resource.

The idea is simple. You only need to assess where you are and what you do, and whether or not your job is a mainstream contributor to the profitability of the organisation. So in case you discover or realise that you are not in the most conducive place for speedy career-growth, there are two ways in which you can align yourself with the high-potential opportunities around you. First, and the one that suits both new-comers and experienced professionals alike, is to move to a department or even another organisation, where you are sure your existing specialisation or expertise will be valued more – like the creative designer who moved from a law firm to an advertising agency and eventually became a famous creative director! If you are a software engineer, look for a company where IT is the central or core business. There is little merit in being the IT-Manager of a hotel. There is only so much you can grow as a support function. If you are a lawyer, go work in a law firm. In most cases you will grow faster at a place where legal prowess is the key driver of revenue. It will always be a better place than to be the legal officer of a fertiliser company.

The second way to propel yourself into a higher growth orbit is more challenging and is more suited to people who have not fully crystallised their area of expertise. For those of us who have been generalists so far, doing different kinds of jobs. So there is no real need to fundamentally re-think your area of specialisation (which could be the case if someone has many years of experience in a certain field) and it will be easier to zero down on a fast-track career line. The same holds true if you are just about starting-out in your career. That is a great place to be. You can allocate some self-development time to yourself on weekends, do some research, meet some people and figure out what opportunities are available to you that match your temperament and are also high-potential in terms of growth. A lot of people discover a bit late in life that they have a flair for selling or for designing or even technology. So identify your race-track, kiss the mud and jump right in!

I will close this chapter with words of caution and encouragement. It will be great if this discussion has helped you measure yourself on the career scale, and if it has energised you to make the necessary changes to go after success like never before. However, it is important to understand that sometimes stability and loyalty become your best pair of wheels on the road to success and you may not want to disturb that. Don't try and change things unless you truly feel that the change is the missing link from your story.

> The biggest risk is not taking any risks. In a world changing really quickly, the only strategy that is guaranteed to fail is not taking any risks.
>
> \- Mark Zuckerberg

On the other hand, don't be too resistant to change either. Don't plant yourself in one place or one kind of job just because it is familiar and comfortable. The only real way to grow in life is to challenge yourself continuously, and emerge as the winner every time. Cast a tougher you in the furnace of your ambition. Give it everything – every drop of sweat, blood and tear. Take a few risks, but make sure the ripples of your determination mitigate most of it. Live your life like a true champion. Like a true *30-something CEO*.

And remember – eventually what wins is not the job or the company or the industry or the specialisation. It is you. You win.

> Success is a science;
> if you have the conditions, you get the result.
>
> – Oscar Wilde

the 360 degree manifesto

Because success is never an accident

We will be lying to ourselves if we talk about success and failure in isolation of some very intimate pieces of our lives. The race-track is not entirely in the professional realm only. It is not about working harder and smarter in office. Preparing yourself to become a *30-something CEO* is a complex, sustained and all-encompassing endeavour. It is not only about what you are going to be doing on one sorted slice of your life – your work. No. It is a lot more than that. Societal and financial excellence is never the outcome of a piecemeal and fragmented life-building approach. It is not something that you do for a few hours or days of your weeks and months. It is about a long-term transformation in your way-of-life and in your very belief-system. It is a 360-degree manifesto that your ambition inks for itself.

In this chapter, I will try to share a few insider truths with you. Some secrets that people seldom talk about. Some lesser-known aspects of a winner's hidden life, but those that play a profound role in deciding ultimate success or failure. We will together journey deep into *the 30-something CEOs'* hearts and minds, homes and lives. And I am sure you will see how being an extraordinary winner takes a lot more than what is visible at the surface. It takes sacrifices and choices that are far harder than anything we have spoken about so far. It takes everything.

> The time I burned my guitar it was like a sacrifice. You sacrifice the things you love. I love my guitar.
>
> – Jimi Hendrix

As a result of what we have discussed in the previous chapters, your mind might be filled with some very logical questions. I have asked you to give everything you have in the pursuit of your goals, to work on weekends (when needed), to stretch the boundaries and outperform everyone around you by sheer grit and commitment, to spend out-of-office time with your corporate militia and more. So you might be wondering, *"Okay I get it that I should put in every ounce of my energy into this quest. But then, how will I take out time for my spouse?"* Or you could be thinking, *"If I devote my weekends to get ahead of my competitors, when do I take my wife for the movies? She's gonna kill me!"* You are right. If you try to bring about a sudden shift in the equilibrium, there probably will be trouble.

There could be other doubts and queries as well. I have spoken about you taking calculated risks, becoming an entrepreneur if you find yourself suitable, or working for start-ups and smaller companies... to name a few. Here, the questions would be quite like this, *"How will I meet my monthly expenses if I take the entrepreneurial leap? Who will pay the rent?"*. Many more similar considerations would raise their heads, *"How can I work for a start-up? Will this not bring in financial unpredictability? How will I pay my EMIs if I lose my job?"* And these are all very fair questions that must be answered.

But *can* these be answered in theory? Is there any fool-proof formula for risk-management? Can the dynamics within a family be discussed over a few pages of *gyaan*? I say this because at the end of the day the reality of your circumstances will play a definitive role in shaping your future. It is like saying that you cannot hope to win a Formula One race if you are driving a 1974

Premier Padmini car. Or that you cannot climb the Everest with a 150-kilogram backpack strapped to your shoulders. No matter how much drive and devotion you have, these circumstantial shortcomings will weigh you down and will not allow you to hit top gear. It works equally the other way round. What if you were barefoot before embarking upon a 20-kilometre marathon and someone quietly slipped top-quality running shoes on your feet? Imagine yourself struggling in sweltering heat and someone switching on an air conditioner you never knew existed? Our careers are no different. There is a near perfect juxtaposition of one's personal and professional lives that must get aligned before someone successfully takes the leap towards extraordinary fame and prosperity.

So what game-changing circumstances am I talking about? What role do these play in our careers? Do we choose the environment around ourselves or is it something that is thrust upon us? Can something be done to avoid the negative stimulus and attract the positive ones? Can circumstances be changed? And most importantly – *do we have a choice?*

> It is our choices…that show what we truly are, far more than our abilities.
>
> – JK Rowling

We always have a choice. Sometimes totally, sometimes partially. But we always have a choice. Some of us are awakened to this fact much sooner in life, and that helps us chart our course of life better by making the right choices. Others among us bump into these realities when it is a bit late. A *bit* late mind you, because it is never too late. Never too late to become a *30-something CEO*.

Let us now dive straight-in and talk about how the choices we make in our personal lives eventually make an unexpectedly profound impact on our professional success or failure. Please note that these views are only my observations and not universally applicable rules. I urge you to not base any life-decisions on what you have read or are about to read. Finally, it is your own wisdom and understanding of the world that should drive all your decisions. You may take my words as just another input among the many others you receive from various sources.

The money plant

Money doesn't grow on trees. It grows on compound interest. It grows in real estate. It grows in interest, incomes and rental pools. It grows if you plant the money-seed at the right time. Believe me, there is no tree that provides better shade than the money-tree.

Yet, most people turn a blind eye to this universally established truth.

> I'd like to live as a poor man with lots of money.
>
> - Pablo Picasso

I know this person, Palash (name changed), since many years now. I would not say he is a close friend, but he is certainly someone I have a lot of fondness for. He made an impression on me the very first time we met, when he was trying to sell a packaged software to my company. I admired his technology prowess as well as his aggressive sales style. We remained in touch for several years, working together on projects off and on. During these interactions, we developed great mutual respect and enjoyed each other's company. As we spent more time together, I discovered one peculiar (at least to me!) habit in Palash. He spent everything he earned. Every penny. And sometimes more. Initially, I couldn't believe it as I was exactly the reverse. I still am. But it was true. He was a brutal money-spender.

This discovery became more and more painful for me as I could not stand the sight of him burning away his monthly pay on unnecessary gizmos, travel and partying. He would upgrade his very expensive mobile phone for the next expensive mobile phone within three months. He had to have the latest laptop, the latest camera, the latest watch and so on. He would travel overseas at the drop of a hat, to wish a friend on her birthday. He was out partying at chic joints every weekends and sometimes, even weekdays. After a while, I couldn't take it any more on a life-principle level. Here I was seeing a friend throwing away precious money and I could not remain a silent spectator. I went ahead and spoke to him. When I casually raised the topic of saving money, he laughed it off saying money was meant to be spent. And that when he would need more, he will earn more. Had he been a younger brother, I would have kicked his backside and forced him to change his way of thinking and his habits. But he was not my younger brother. All I could do was protest a little and laugh along.

A couple of years later, he came to me for advice. The Indian start-up environment had become very favourable for entrepreneurs and he wanted to take up the position of a co-founder in a high-quality venture. I encouraged him as I could see that particular start-up was founded by a credible entrepreneur and had great potential. Palash sadly confessed that he was worried about his financial situation, in case something went wrong with the start-up. The fact remains that risk exists even for the most promising of new companies and I could not reassure him on that front. Finally, he took the worst decision of his career – he gave up the opportunity to be co-founder of that company. And he did it because he could not sustain himself without a regular income even for two months. His bank account was empty. That was what had forced him to abandon his life's greatest growth opportunity without even a fight.

Was his decision an outcome of his circumstances, or did he create those circumstances for himself?

Do you think he would have been riding the start-up train as co-founder of a great company, had he been more financially responsible? Think of what his decision might have been, if he had enough in his bank to sustain him for just 6 months, should the rainy day have arrived? However, he was compelled to change the very course of his career and his life simply because he didn't create the right conditions for his success.

Yes, *conditions* for success. That is what this discussion is about.

We have discussed many things so far in this book. Hard-work, enterprise (we will discuss it more in the next chapter), risk-appetite, team-building, sacrifice and so much more. But what we have not spoken about so far is that none of these can work effectively if they are exerted in isolation. Extraordinary success comes only when exceptional effort merges forces with a larger preparedness framework. And, financial preparedness is among the primary factors that make a difference.

If you remember, I had mentioned earlier that during late 2015, I stepped down from a CEO position in a multinational firm to start my company Talentrack. You might also recollect me saying that I had a very impressive pay packet. Now tell me, how do you think I was able to let go of such lucrative compensation and start a company where I was not going to get even a fraction of the salary? The answer is simple. It was not because I was a hero. It was because I was prepared. And I had been preparing for over one and a half decades.

> Frugality includes all the other virtues.
>
> – Cicero

My father taught me the virtues of saving money when I was just a child. I can say with full conviction that I am who I am today largely because of my father's teachings. But what I thank him for most is that he taught me the importance of saving *early* in life. He would say, *"Make compound interest your friend early in life. When responsibilities kick-in, marriage, children, school fees, loans... everyone is forced to save. But by then it is rather late and the saving-potential becomes lower. Save when you have no real responsibilities. Save and become rich before you are 30!"* He showed me the way towards becoming a *30-something CEO*. When I started earning from my first job in GE, I used to come back home and handover my entire salary to my dad, who would then invest it wisely on my behalf. In fact, he would give me pocket-money like he used to when I was in college, so my salary could be 100 per cent saved! When my colleagues at work were busy buying imported jeans and watches, I was watching my money grow. I bought my first plot of land when I was 23, and a huge three-floor house when I was 26. Most of my colleagues who were buying watches and scotch from their first-job, haven't bought one yet.

So when I stepped-down from the CEO position, I had built enough financial cushion to last my family and me a lifetime or more of very comfortable living. I was not dependent on a salary, so was free to take bold decisions. So it was not my pure-play enterprise or reckless self-belief that made me do it. I was able to do it because of years of discipline and preparation that had been underway, and provided me with the requisite springboard.

Believe me, it was a very well-planned and conscious way-of-life. I drove smaller cars when I could buy much flashier ones. I would dine at mediocre restaurants when I could easily afford the finest in town. As a family and as an individual, we knew financial strength kicks-in like a body-armour when you need it the most. Financial weakness raises its head just when you can least afford it.

A *30-something CEO* knows that radical growth will not be possible unless radical decisions are taken. The old dusty career-path treaded upon by millions will not lead to unusual success and glory. Some non-traditional, even risky routes will have to be taken to circumvent a 25-year long success-journey and shorten it to a decade. When this knowledge is clear and present, *the 30-something CEO* does not sleep over it. He starts working on it.

Most of us believe that our youth years are meant to be enjoyed and hence burning away our early years' incomes is justified. To this I would say, what worth is youth if it takes *money* for it to be enjoyed?! It is so easy to *udaao* money and feel rich temporarily. The truth is that the difference between the saver and the spender starts becoming visible in five years' time. And it becomes a yawning gap in ten years. The depth and security of a saver outweigh the spender's lifestyle in no time, and over a period of time, they look like they come from different brackets of society. More than that, saving in your twenties paves way for an exceptionally secure thirties, which in turn drives greater value than you can imagine. It paves way for the emergence of a *30-something CEO.*

Let's go back to Palash's life. Now imagine if he had not frittered away his hefty salary in unnecessary *show-sha*, and had saved 30-40 per cent of his income from the day he started earning. It was very possible. He lived with his parents, like most of us *acchha-bacchas* do in this part of the world. He was not married, didn't have to run a household and even drove his dad's second car! Can there be any justification for him to not have saved and invested wisely? Now consider a situation where he had accumulated rupees ten lakhs over the years. Now go back to his decision about joining the start-up as a co-founder. What do you think would have happened? He would have jumped on to the bandwagon and who knows he might have been a multimillionaire today. As I know, he is still driving his dad's second car. He is still waiting to upgrade his iPhone 6 as soon as his next pay cheque comes in.

So what is it that you need to do to make sure that this pre-condition for success holds true for you? You could be an engineering student or you could be someone with twenty years of work behind you. Be that as it may, you can start *now*. Of course, the newer you are in the race, the more chances you will get. Even if you have limited saving-potential, don't get disheartened. The first thing you have got to do is to start looking at your savings not as a safety-belt, but as an engine, as a facilitator. Most importantly – as a liberator! When you look at it positively, it will energise you to work harder and enjoy every moment.

Since this book is not about personal financial management, it is beyond the scope of this chapter to discuss the various simple and complex aspects of saving and investment. However, I cannot help but emphasise the importance of personal wealth-creation as a potent tool and almost a pre-condition for your journey towards becoming a *30-something CEO*.

If marriages are made in Heaven, companies are built in Hell!

When I proposed to my beautiful wife Munisha, I said to her, "*Will you be my second wife?*" She obviously didn't find this statement romantic, and frowned at what I was saying. She probably wanted to punch me. So I quickly added, "*...because you know I am already married to Magnon, my company!*" She knew me well. She had known me for years and had seen my struggles in building my company. She knew I was devoted to succeeding professionally, and that was probably one of the very few things she admired about me! She laughed and said yes. *Phew!*

There is a reason why I am sharing a very personal moment of my life with you. There is an important message I want to get across. Why do you think I proposed the way I did? Why did I have to spoil one of the most special occasions of my life? There was a reason. And the reason was that I wanted my future life-partner to grasp the importance of my career and company for me very unambiguously. I was very clear that my wife's partnership would be mission-critical towards the achievement of my aspirations. If I had married someone who did not fully appreciate this unflappable zeal, we were going to have a problem. Either I would not have been able to nurture my dream the way I wanted to, or I would have failed in building the marriage I so cared for. This was a trade-off I could never get myself into. Just the way she knew me for years, I knew her too. I was convinced that she was on-board with me on this flight. She knew she would have to make sacrifices and she was ready for it. In all these years, she has not gone back on that promise. She goes for very few holidays with me because I take very few days off. She represents us at most family get-togethers because I am mostly in team or business dinners at that time. Even as I write these words, there is a T20 India-Pakistan match going-on on TV. I am writing away all alone in my study, while she is watching the match in the bedroom. The truth is, she is the real *30-something CEO.*

Today, I would not have been where I am had it not been for Munisha's undying and boundless support. She has only added reasons for me to succeed. Now I want to succeed for her.

Enough about me. Let me tell you about Mayank (name changed), a very dear friend of mine. He is my *bachpan ka saathi.* He has always been a brilliant and ambitious person, and he is an engineer with and an MBA. He was not as crazy as I was, but he wanted to win in life. He started his career well and was also good at building strong relationships at work. In fact, everyone loved Mayank. He was also a great saver of money and had built quite a kitty till. Till that day. That day he decided to get married to this charming girl. Everything changed post after that.

Mayank's greatest role in life now is that of a husband. He is consumed in making his marriage work, fulfilling the never-ending emotional and financial demands of his wife – In pacifying her because she is always angry, and in completing household chores that she refuses to do. She does not work and is a home-maker. Of course, nothing wrong with that. But she wants the finest things in life. She also wants her husband at her beck and call. She wants him to become a millionaire quickly, and spares no opportunity in making that vociferously clear. To add to this, he has to also entertain her throughout the weekend with movies, dinners, trips, etc. She wants him to buy big cars and big houses like some of his friends, but also wants him back home on time every single day. She wants him enthusiastically present at all her family functions, but sulks and insults people at his office gatherings. She calls and texts him twenty times when he is at work, and not with loving messages. He tries hard, and she keeps making it harder for him. She humiliates him for his financial constraints, but doesn't give him a day of peace to focus on his work and career. He has now even stopped thinking about success. He is simply just a husband now. And not a happy one at that.

> What's with this domestic stuff? Tend to business, will ya?
>
> – Mickey Goldmill, Rocky II

Mayank is not alone in this tough space. We have this supremely capable manager in our company called Anjali (name changed), who was meant for big things. Till a while back, she was a go-getter and hungry for success. Anjali was the top revenue-earner of the region and was winning loads of accolades. Eventually her husband began to develop a complex and made her life miserable. She was prohibited from staying even a minute extra in office, and summarily barred from attending agency parties. She does not work with me directly but from what I hear from my colleagues she is no longer the tiger she was. She is subdued, eats her meals alone and is quiet in most team meetings. Her performance is still okay, but nowhere close to what she used to be. She could have been a *30-something CEO*. She will probably retire as a Senior Manager many years from now.

Please get this right. I am a great believer in the institution of marriage. For me, it is a sacrosanct bond between a couple. So please do not interpret anything I say even remotely as a rant against marriage. Like I have said before, I myself could not have seen the little success I have had, had it not been for the partnership of my wife at every step. Some of the richest and most famous people in the world are committed family persons, be it the *baadshah* of Bollywood Shahrukh Khan or the steel magnate LN Mittal. Be it the powerful billionaire Mukesh Ambani or the cricket legend Sachin Tendulkar himself. Be it Kareena Kapoor Khan or Kiran Mazumdar Shaw... they are all in great marriages. So there is no question of undermining the importance of relationships and spouses. Which is precisely why you cannot insulate your career from your partner. They are deeply interconnected.

This connect is something that most people don't pay enough attention to, which is a mistake. It can sometimes be the only mistake one makes in life, but can end up paying the price in perpetuity. If there is a significant and unexpected mismatch in what you expect from life and what your partner hopes to get, there are bound to be problems. The point to note here is that most of the times, it is nobody's mistake. If you don't make it amply clear to your partner as to how much your success and career mean to you, how can you expect him or her to understand your journey, let alone support it? And it does not hold true only for married couples. It is equally crucial if you are in a relationship with someone and you think this might be for keeps.

Peace in your relationship and support from your partner are extremely vital conditions for a *30-something CEO* to stretch his legs and sprint towards the pinnacle of achievement. There are very few people who are able to keep home and office exclusive of each other. It is not a natural thing to do. Happiness at home brings prosperity at work, and vice versa. A great day at work would usually end with a loving evening of fun and laughter at home. A bitter fight with a spouse will always cast a dark shadow on your work day. It is a reality of life. Naturally, when this interdependence is so central to our career, why is it not talked about? Our parents teach us to be very selective in the kind of jobs we pick or the institutions we study in. Then why not also educate us on this serious matter? Why is it not taught in schools?

I think no one raises this game-changing topic because it can be politically incorrect. I was advised by my colleagues not to write about it, which is precisely why I am devoting an entire section to it. We cannot keep this elephant under wraps. We must not do it. This spouse-career dynamic impacts millions of people every day. It builds or destroys homes and careers. It has the power to change destinies for good. So why should such a topic not be analysed and studied? Should it not be understood by everyone in our society so that people make informed choices on what will profoundly influence their lives? To put it simply, if Mayank and Anjali had time-machines or crystal-balls where they could have foreseen their future, would they have still stuck to the choices they made? I don't think so. And I think we owe it to each other to have this discussion in an uncomplicated and positive way.

Either a dreamer goes solo and does not take a spouse or partner ever or at least not during the formative years. While I cannot criticise this approach vehemently as many people choose to live this way, I don't support this path as it seems too imbalanced, too extreme. Which means most of us will need to find that precious equilibrium between our homes and companies. Again, please bear in mind that when I say 'most of us', I am referring to the ambitious among us. The ones who are burning with the desire to become *30-something CEOs*. This whole discussion becomes diluted when it comes to mediocre people who don't expect much from life. They are okay with a mundane job as long as it pays the rent, drives the car and buys movie tickets on the weekends. I am not talking about that section of the society.

There was a scene in the beautiful Hindi movie *Zindagi Na Milegi Dobara* that set me thinking. It shows the ever-dashing Hrithik Roshan's character in a heated argument with his girlfriend. In that scene, he tries to tell her how his meeting with the leader of a top corporation will help boost his career in a big way. To this, she yells back that they have had to cancel a holiday for this meeting of his. He goes on to explain that they can plan a holiday anytime, but he would never get the chance to meet this top shot again. His girlfriend responds to this point in the most dramatic way by reminding him that it was her birthday during their originally planned holiday, and that her birthday won't come again. They break-up.

> The question isn't who is going to let me; it's who is going to stop me.
>
> – Ayn Rand

I could not help but go over this scene over and over again. It was a terrific capture of the reality between several couples today. I did not know whom to side with because both characters had equally passionate arguments – though I did find a technical flaw in the girl saying her birthday won't come again. It will come every year, sweety! And also that your boyfriend is able to afford these fancy holidays for you simply because he is a work-tiger and makes enough dough! It is also the other way round. Being a huge fan of the American television serial *Friends*, I can recollect almost every episode from every season. Yes, I have a life too *yaar*! I remember this episode where Rachel (played by the gorgeous Jennifer Aniston) is accosted by her boyfriend Ross (played by the handsome David Schwimmer) for not spending enough time with him because she is too busy with her job. To this, Rachel retorts that for the first time in her life she has a job that she loves and one she is good at, and that Ross should accept and respect that. So it is really about what people want from their lives, and about finding a partner who blends into the plan seamlessly as a big strength, rather than as a permanent impediment.

My advice to the young, unhitched readers of this book is that you look for life-partners like a determined entrepreneur looks for a co-founder. Look for someone who shares your dreams, has similar life-goals, is ready to make sacrifices and has the traits of a dependable partner. Because just like a co-founder decides the fate of a company either way, a spouse seals the boundaries of your destiny. I have heard all those *pyaar kiya nahin jaata, ho jaata hai* drama, and disagree completely. It is your whole life at stake. Your dreams, your ambitions, your promises... everything. You cannot let everything be compromised just because you fail to see the powerful link between the health of your relationship and the wellness of your career. Whoever you are going to tie that eternal bond with, make sure you let them know in no unclear words what support you expect from them. Be yourself and live the life you plan to live – and let them observe it. If they are okay with it totally and happily, go for it.

If you are someone who is already in a marriage or a relationship and you feel a bit held back in your career because of relationship obligations, don't worry. Nothing is lost. You can bring about a change in your life the day you decide to. At the end of the day, your spouse loves you and cares for you. Your spouse ultimately wants to see you happy. But you will have to make a beginning. You will have to bring this issue out in the open, and have the courage to discuss it candidly with your partner. The important thing to understand here is that we may want to win a bit for ourselves, but the satisfaction of a victory is most when it is shared with our loved ones. What happiness will you get in buying a flashy Mercedes Benz if you don't drive it home to someone? What is the excitement of buying a big house, if there is no one to share it with you? We know we want to win for our loved ones. I think they will understand it very well too, once we explain it to them. They would want to be our partners on this exciting journey – but we will have to invite them to it.

Communication is the biggest strength or the greatest weakness, depending on how you position it in your relationship. Look at your spouse as a difficult yet indispensable co-founder or key employee. What do we do in those cases? We talk. We make the co-founder or key-employee see our viewpoint. We keep working on them till we make some headway. If we can do it at work, we can do the same at home.

> Mumkin hai safar ho aasaan…
>
> – Ghazal sung by Suresh Wadkar (Doordarshan)

Before I draw a close to this subject, allow me to submit once again that my reason for writing on this mostly taboo topic is because I deeply respect relationships. I have personally witnessed lives getting made or destroyed as an outcome of one's home dynamics. Just remember this is one of the essential pre-conditions for an exceptional success story. Unquestioned support and understanding of your partner is like the pair of running-shoes before the marathon or the air-conditioner in the sweaty room. It makes the journey so much easier.

Think about it. You have a partner who stands by you like a pillar, no matter what. She walks shoulder to shoulder with you, come success or failure. And you have enough money in the bank to see your upkeep through for a year, without having to beg, borrow or steal. Is there any dream you cannot chase with these munitions backing you?

There is very little in this world that a heart full of love and a pocket full of cash cannot achieve together.

Any great warrior is also a scholar, and a poet, and an artist.

– Steven Seagal

nine essential traits of

The 30-something CEO

"Take up one idea. Make that one idea your life – think of it, dream of it, live on that idea. Let the brain, muscles, nerves, every part of your body be full of that idea, and just leave every other idea alone. That is the way to success.

– Swami Vivekananda

We now come to the last chapter of this book, which I enjoyed writing the most. Here I want to share with you some very key and common qualities I have noticed in several super-successful people I have worked with or observed over the years. I don't think I have met anyone who has ALL these traits to the fullest, but most of these are found in some measure or the other in all self-made, supremely successful people. And I truly believe you will benefit from getting a good grasp on each of these traits.

What is even more important to note here is that almost none of these traits are anything that a person is born with. While we cannot totally reject the idea of some people being naturally gifted with certain specific talents or skills, the qualities of the *30-something CEOs* that I am describing here are mostly acquired and sharpened with years of practice, discipline and focus. We see sports stars and their training grind is visible. You can see them living in the gyms, burning sweat and pushing their limits. It is enormously inspiring to see them. What we don't realise is that business champions also have their own routine. They also live by a discipline that is rare and punishing, but is unfortunately not visible to the observer's common eye. It is a grilling routine that they set for themselves, a fierce pace, but it is all hidden behind the closed doors of their offices, studies and airport lounges.

Their output is not measurable in terms of six-pack abs on glossy magazine covers or in their field athleticism. It manifests itself in very many forms that are not easily traceable by a common observer. And because it is not something everyone can see, many times we give credit to their luck and stars for their extraordinary achievements.

I am here to break that mind-set. I am here to show you the reality, the pain and the indomitable will that fuel every success story. I am here to tell you what it is that winners do quietly but persistently, that makes them stand apart. It is my sincere hope that you will study each of these traits with a view to inculcate and imbibe them in your own life.

Let's take a look at these essential qualities now. They are not given in any order of importance. Each one is as vital as the other.

1. Enterprise

> It had long since come to my attention that people of accomplishment rarely sat back and let things happen to them. They went out and happened to things.
>
> – Leonardo da Vinci

I was once addressing a large group of people that had filled the auditorium to capacity. It was a session with final semester

MBA students. My lecture was an hour long, after which there were scores of hands that shot up to ask questions. One of them reminded me of a statement I had made during the discourse – *"a lot of people work hard and stay committed, yet they fail to achieve success to their full potential"*. He looked exasperated when he asked me, *"If hard-work and commitment also don't guarantee success, what more can anyone do?"* It was a logical question and I remember how I pounced on it with a one-word reply – *"Enterprise!"*

This is the question most people fail to ask. During the course of your lifetime you will see hundreds of people who work very hard, stay persistent and yet are unable to reach for the sky. Of course, such people can never remain complete failures and will definitely achieve some degree of success sooner or later, but in numerous cases it is not the best they could have got. So what holds them back? It is the same one-word answer – enterprise.

What *is* enterprise? How is it different from hard-work? Well, it is very different. Hard-work is the main ingredient during the preparation of the dish called success. Nothing much can be achieved without it. However, there are many other ingredients that go into the dish to turn it into a delicacy – or super-achievement. These ingredients are perseverance, humility, intelligence… to name a few. Then comes the secret sauce. The secret that is known only to the master chefs or *the 30-something CEOs*. And that secret sauce is *enterprise.*

Enterprise has a very rich and profound meaning. You might

have heard people describing somebody saying *"She is very enterprising and gets what she wants"*. To put it simply, enterprise is the ability to think and act differently in the pursuit of one's goals. It is the capability to create opportunities where none exists and to go after them with a rigorous and unconventional approach. It is a combined term for goal-seeking, problem-solving, creativity and out-of-the-box thinking. And when hard-work, intelligence, humility and perseverance are sprinkled with the rich sauce of enterprise – the result is an extraordinary winner.

Whether it is about getting admission into a foreign university, or being able to get an interview with that successful CEO, or being able to impress venture capital firms with your novel business idea, or being the first to get the coveted promotion, or earning useful degrees while working full-time or just about anything that provides unusual acceleration to your career, it will require enterprise of some form or the other. A mediocre manager may say *"I will work hard for that Vice President promotion"*, and I admire that deeply. However, a manager with enterprise may say *"I will work hard for that Vice President promotion, network with the right people in the company, make sure my contribution gets noticed, and will also present some path-breaking ideas in the next meeting with the CEO"*. Get the point?

2. Cast-in-stone resilience

> The difference between winning and losing is most often not quitting.
>
> – Walt Disney

Resilience, in my opinion, is a complicated concept. We refer to the person who has stuck to his guns even in the darkest of times, as resilient. What we perhaps don't realise is that sometimes that person has no other option but to carry on. What looks like a great feat to an outsider, is really the only option the individual has and all he does is follows the only path available to him. But when he emerges a winner, people say he has resilience. I once heard a similar view point in a brilliant interview by the great Amitabh Bachchan, and could not help but admire him even more. As a corollary, resilience will always be lower when an escape route is available, right?

What successful people do is that they convince themselves that they have no escape route available, no choice left. No choice but to go on, fight on, no matter what. And, it is this self-suggestion and self-discipline that eventually makes all the difference.

The truth is that abandoning a post is always an option. Scrapping a project is always a choice. Escaping pressure (or combatting it!) is a natural reaction for everyone. We have to make a choice between fight or flight. We are faced with this dilemma many times in our lives. It is such moments that differentiate between a winner from a commoner. When the *Senior Manager for Life* decides to quit a high-pressure job or run away from an entrepreneurial project, *the 30-something CEO* fastens his seatbelts, grinds his teeth and prepares for an even harder fight. He does not give up.

> “ Courage is grace under pressure.
>
> – Ernest Hemingway

I was once approached by a young aspiring entrepreneur who wanted me to be an angel investor in his start-up. He was a great guy, an electronics engineer, a management graduate, smart, suave, ambitious and soft-spoken. Within ten minutes of meeting him, I decided in my mind, to invest in his venture. Only until he made a statement that ended the conversation in my mind that very second, and the whole meeting, within three minutes. As he described how he was ready to face withstand failure, he said, *“I have decided to give it all I have for two years. If it doesn't work even after that, I will try to return your money and go get a job”.* The decision was taken. Despite all his smartness and capability, I would never invest in him. Instead, if he had only said that come what may, he would stick to his entrepreneurial dream and devote his life to it, he would have left the room with a big investment cheque!

Please understand this point well. You will seldom succeed at anything, any job, any assignment, any start-up, any role – if you plan your escape routes first. Ever thought where the phrase *'burning all your bridges'* might have come from? It would have probably come from a valiant military general who would have, on his own volition, ordered all retreat routes to be destroyed, so that he had no choice left but to battle head-on. You will have to do the same in your life and career. I don't have to repeat the stories of great people who fought for years with success evading them, before eventually creating history – Henry Ford, Steve Jobs, Howard Hughes, Richard Branson, Shiv Nadar and more. This is true not only for the business community, but for everyone as well – sportsmen, writers, actors, film-makers, lawyers and anyone seeking the pinnacles of success.

Remember it is easy to stay motivated for a few days or weeks or months, till some real problems and hurdles spring up. The most inspiring quality of most super-achievers I have met till date is that they have erased the word 'escape' from their dictionaries. They don't know what that means. I have seen these extraordinary people facing several storms simultaneously and yet moving forward unstoppably. You will see them entangled in a legal battle on one end, lose important business orders on the other, face a cash-crunch at the same time and be loaded with strenuous targets – all at once. Yet, they battle-on like a warrior who is surrounded in the field by several adversaries, and does not give up. He believes he will win. You believe he will win.

> He who desired to surge forward even in the face of raining fire;
>
> He whose victory appeared possible even when unarmed & surrounded by the enemy.
>
> – Shyam Narayan Pandey, Haldighati (translated)

Whichever professional field you might be in and whatever you want to do to become an exceptional winner, resilience or the ability to withstand pressure, failure, criticism and hardship without losing steam is crucial for success. If you have decided to become an IAS officer, go after it like it is the last thing you are going to be doing on this planet. If you don't succeed at first, try again. Harder. If you aim to become a world-famous chef, don't let anything hold you back, no matter how many times you fail. If you run a small business that has stagnated over the years, don't let that corrode your enthusiasm. Work even harder than before, and this time, with enterprise on your side.

Don't stop. Don't slow down. Don't give up. You are the only one who can stop you.

3. He is a social animal

> Friends are the best to turn to when you're having a rough day.
>
> – Justin Bieber

As we mentioned in the chapter about building our corporate militia, off-office socialising, bonding and networking are absolutely imperative when you are aiming to be supremely successful.

Take the case of Robin Hood again (I love him!). He was as much a party-thrower as he was a bandit leader. His love for archery contests with his mates was matched equally by his love for guzzling ale with them around a bonfire. Why only Robin of Locksley? Most men and women who succeed in this highly connected world are people who know how to get along with others, inspire others and build strong teams. They may or may not be universally popular, but the people who work with them closely trust them blindly. This trust does not germinate only by being in office together or by meeting in conference rooms or at the water coolers. A relationship of mutual respect, admiration, laughter and collective dreaming comes only when it is nurtured carefully. Little wonder that the most successful people in this world know this secret intuitively.

I once met a senior corporate leader who was the Asia Chairman of his company. He was an Indian and had worked his way up towards a powerful global role. He had at least seven countries (markets) under him, thousands of people under his leadership and was an icon in his industry. We met for breakfast at the Breach Candy Club in Mumbai. He was accompanied by his CFO. We could have easily had the meeting at his office or mine, but he had insisted we meet for a meal. The three of us met and I was delighted to witness the hospitality and genuine affection with which this senior leader cared for not just me, but his CFO as well. At first, he suggested we sit at the best table next to the sea rocks, recommended the delicious all-day breakfast with bacon & eggs, fussed about minor details like whether I preferred marmalade or butter on my toast and more. By the time we finished breakfast, he had totally won my friendship! What was noteworthy was that he was not so warm and hospitable only with me, but also with the CFO who had worked with him for years. It simply showed me how he genuinely liked and respected people. How he knew we would never find the same chemistry in a closed office meeting room.

If you are working somewhere already, you will probably see two kinds of people in your office. The first kind just wait for the clock to strike 5.30 pm and they pick up their bags and head for the train home. Most of them do the same even on a Friday. They find their coming to office enough to keep their careers flying. I strongly feel that they are making a mistake. The second kind are the ones who look for friends at work. They are the ones that make the quickest cricket-match plans, the Friday evening beer gathering or the Sunday bar-be-cue at a senior colleague's patio. All this starts with the pleasant intention of having a good time together, but it soon transforms into close friendships. I have seen this happen more than once. With some luck, eventually this bunch metamorphoses into a corporate militia.

> A man's friendships are one of the best measures of his worth.
>
> – Charles Darwin

These bonding and off-office hours are useful even with people outside your immediate working group. These hours can be used to spend quality time with your clients. They can be utilised beautifully in networking with media persons or bureaucrats. You could start cultivating a relationship with a future investor for your business. The point is, don't make the mistake of thinking that work-battles are confined to work hours and office premises. They are fought as much outside it as inside, if not more. When you keep yourself aloof from this end of the action, don't be disappointed if you miss out on some great opportunities that could have come your way. That is because when your boss first spoke about that opportunity over a Sunday lunch, your competitor was there to listen to him. You were not.

I have been a people's person throughout my career. The reality is that I don't have to make an effort to spend time with my colleagues and friends. I love them as much as one would love a family, and I enjoy their company as much as one enjoys the presence of lifelong friends. So there is no extra effort whatsoever and we are able to create the finest combination of work and pleasure. Some of our most exciting business project ideas emerged when we were enjoying a fine scotch together or when we were out for a game of tennis.

A long time ago, I heard a friend narrate an incident from the life of the great Richard Branson, where Sir Branson spent a long time shut in an apartment, partying with a rock band! He came out of that apartment with a valuable contract for Virgin Music in his hands. See what I am saying?

4. Creativity

They may be hardened CEOs. They may look very boring in those grey business suits. Some of them may be the quietest during team meetings. They might look like bean-counters at all times because all they talk about is numbers. Their appearance may be that of a sharp banker or one of a nerdy engineer. But the one attribute I can guarantee you will find in every exceptionally successful individual, in every *30-something CEO* – is creativity. I can talk about this point with a delightful sense of confidence, because I have led TBWA and Magnon\TBWA in the vast and diverse market that is India, and, TBWA is one of the most creative companies in the whole world.

Creativity is a very broad phenomenon. Different people understand it differently. Some think creativity is what a painter does. Others think product engineers are creative. Some people assume creativity is the bastion of creative organisations like advertising agencies and should be left to them. Others find it in the way a salesman plans his pitch deck. Yet others say that an accountant who presents financial data in any way he desires is a creative genius. All of them are right.

> A person with a new idea is a crank until the idea succeeds.
>
> – Mark Twain

They say Steve Jobs had an uncanny eye for creative excellence in every product that Apple came out with. He took a deep personal interest in the design, user experience and packaging. His search for creative excellence continued even when he worked closely with Pixar, even though the business was completely different. So who was Steve Jobs? A tough businessman or a romantic artist? Howard Hughes, the aviator and among the richest men in the world in his time, was both an aerospace engineer and a film-maker at the same time. Can you imagine how his creative prowess would have stretched from advanced engineering to the glamorous world of celluloid? The simple point is that creativity is not something bound by specialisations or business verticals. It is a human trait. Most importantly, a trait that can be developed by every human.

Yes, creativity can be learnt, nurtured and excelled. No doubt some of us are born with a flair for music or writing or painting or acting, but that is at best a slight advantage. There is no one who became a world-champion on natural talent. Anyone and everyone who has created a name and left a legacy, did it as an outcome of tremendous hard-work, focus and practice. And *the 30-something CEOs* are no different.

Believe me, you are more creative than you think. Agreed,

that most of us don't get the right opportunities and platforms to identify, develop and express our creativity fully in the conventional sense. But it is important to understand that we do get chances to demonstrate our creative intelligence every day at work or study. The awesome presentation you make that is different from the run-of-the-mill stuff your colleagues use – that is creative! Your new business idea that you thought of while sitting with your friends in your college canteen – that is creative. When you come-up with new thoughts about how to sell your products or services more during the festive season, that is creative. When you work with friends to organise the best college festival, that is creative. You see, Uber is creative. Flipkart is creative. Zomato is creative. Snapdeal is creative. Myntra is creative. You are creative!

The 30-something CEOs come up with terrific ideas during workshops. They would send a short text message to their close colleagues even on a Sunday, describing a new strategy that they have bumped into. They will have the best suggestions for the office annual day dinner and they will be the first ones to advice product teams on what will click in the market. Even when they are in boring and traditional businesses like banking or steel manufacturing, they will add a spin to it. Do you know how they do all this? It is not because they are born more creative than you and I. It is because they are always thinking, always on a quest to improve things. To improve their grades if they are in college. To enhance their productivity if they are preparing for a competitive examination. To strengthen their departments if they are leading them. And to expand their businesses if they run them. You cannot keep the creativity of a thinker in a box. Sooner or later, the rich colours of his creative acumen will paint the canvas of whatever he does.

> Creativity is a natural extension of our enthusiasm.
>
> – Earl Nightingale

Just remember, *the 30-something CEO* in you is extremely creative. Don't think of creativity as just art or colours or theatre or writing. Think of creativity as in start-ups, in the path-breaking business ideas that change the world forever. I know I am taking his name for the second time in this book, but that is because I believe in him. Prime Minister Narendra Modi displayed brilliant creativity when he floated the idea of foregoing the LPG subsidy by the well-offs in our country to light a million rural stoves in the process. He was refreshingly creative when he visited the offices of Facebook and spoke to millions of people like a friend, paving way for a visible boost in India's business-friendly image in the world.

He is, in my humble opinion, a *30-something CEO.* And so shall you be the day you so choose.

4. People loving

> "The idea flow from the human spirit is absolutely unlimited. All you have to do is tap into that well. I don't like to use the word efficiency. It's creativity. It's a belief that every person counts.
>
> - Jack Welch

In my second book, *The Street to the Highway*, I wrote a chapter with perhaps the most complicated and yet the simplest title in the world. It was called 'People'. This topic deserves not a chapter, not a book but a whole Encyclopedia series written on it. Given the scope of my book, I think I made a good beginning, for it is now beyond doubt that people make or break the fortunes of a company.

There are always exceptions, but I don't seem to have met or read about any super-achiever who did not like people. Please understand, there is a difference in being a loner and in not liking people. The king of pop, Michael Jackson was known to be a loner, but his friends knew he absolutely adored people. People adored him. There can be successful men and women who like their moments of peace and quiet, but deep down they all really admire and love the people around them.

Today, I can say it with complete honesty that I would not have achieved even a fraction of the success I have seen in life, had it not been for the team I have around me for over a decade and a half. They truly made all the difference! They fought by my side when I needed strength. They encouraged me when the chips were down. They held fort when I was away. They rejoiced with me at all my triumphs without envy. They stood by me during all my failures without losing their respect for me. They supported my ideas yet questioned me rigorously at every step. They followed my instructions but held their own decision-making fully intact. We learnt together, evolved together and built institutions together. Today, we are not just business partners. We love each other like family.

In your quest to grab a piece of the sky, you must acknowledge the presence of people. You must understand that you will grow the fastest and the surest when you grow collectively. You have to appreciate that there is only one gold-standard investment in this world – and that is the investment into people. The relationships you build will be your assets throughout your journey.

Let me give you the most recent example from my own story. As I have mentioned before, I started my new company Talentrack in 2015. After founding and leading the Magnon Group for 16 years (and leading them even today), this was my first independent entrepreneurial venture since the year 2000. At Talentrack, we envisioned a change in the talent-hiring dynamics of the US$ 18 billion (slated to hit US$ 100 billion by 2025 as per www.ibef.org, Ministry of Commerce & Industry, Government of India) media & entertainment industry forever, and it is an ambitious tech company. Like most start-ups, I needed the two mission-critical resources – financial investment and a high-quality team. I didn't have to look far.

Would you believe it if I tell you that I raised seed-capital for Talentrack even before I wrote the full business plan? And that I did not have to knock on a hundred doors of start-up accelerators, angel funds and high net worth individuals? Will you also believe me if I share that the entire initial team of Talentrack comprised of people known to me? That I did not have to interview and evaluate strangers? This is all true and I have been very fortunate. It was possible because at every step along the way during my 17-year corporate journey, I built real relationships of trust and affection with people both senior and junior to me. So when I went to some of my mentors and superiors with my idea for Talentrack, I found ready investors. That too investors who had complete faith in me. When I started planning the initial team, all I had to do was to pick-up my phone and call some real talented people I have known over the years and invite them to my new company. They jumped at the opportunity. It was more their love for me personally than it was about their confidence in Talentrack. The fact that I was doing it and that I had deep conviction about it was all they needed.

> " Someone is sitting in the shade today because someone planted a tree a long time ago.
>
> – Warren Buffet

The core point here is that when I was building these relationships over the years, I had absolutely no idea that I will one day need investors and teams for a new company, and that these people will so beautifully fit the bill. You can never progress on this path if you have a pre-planned agenda around each individual. It will never allow you to embrace everyone you click with irrespective of whether they are useful to you then or not. A *30-something CEO* loves people, admires them and genuinely works towards building lasting relationships without any immediate incentive to do so. He knows it will all come back one day, with a multiplier effect.

So value people you meet and work with along your journey. Don't leave a company on a bitter note. Don't forget people once they are not of use to you. Send those birthday and anniversary greetings to as many people as you can. Maintain your humility with colleagues you may have outperformed or even had to fire. Share food with your office housekeeping staff once in a while. Treat ex-bosses with more respect than you treated them with when they were your bosses. Remember the names of people's children. It is the thought and energy behind these small things that stay in the universe and wait for the right time to pay you back manifold.

6. Equal effectiveness as a lone-wolf and as a team-player

It is lonely at the top they say. Most leaders who reach the peak of success do feel the pangs of loneliness. It is not loneliness in the social sense that we normally understand. It is the feeling of being alone intellectually and sometimes spiritually. It is a state-of-mind where one greatly misses the presence of honest advisors and fearless sounding-boards. It is a feeling of being alone in both success and failure.

> "Isn't cricket supposed to be a team sport? I feel people should decide first whether cricket is a team game or an individual sport.
>
> – Sachin Tendulkar

On the other hand, most of our formative years are spent in the midst of big and small teams, in delivering group targets and chasing collective goals. Team-work is the buzzword, and rightly so. It is in these years that we learn the art and science of management, when we get educated in group dynamics and become adept in various key aspects of business including communication, execution and result-orientation.

We have all heard statements like *"He is an excellent team-player!"* or *"He is damn good otherwise but struggles when he is in a group…"*. The first statement describes someone who excels when operating in a team. The second one talks about a person who is otherwise a great performer, but loses that excellence when put in a team. Neither of the above two examples is a rarity. We see all sorts of combinations – people who are fantastic superiors but terrible juniors; folks who are excellent teammates but horrible bosses; people who make brilliant second-in-command but become a disaster when asked to lead from the top.

Which of the above is a *30-something CEO*? Is he a team-player or a lone-wolf? Is he a good boss or a wonderful subordinate? Is he better as the top leader or as the next-in-command? Which of the above roles/situations is he exceptionally good at? The answer is – all of the above.

As we have established repeatedly over the content of this book, *the 30-something CEO* is an extraordinary individual, an exceptional talent. Most of the winners I have met till date are able to leverage their exceptional capability wherever they are, in whatever they do. They are efficient and obedient juniors. They make totally dependable and enthusiastic teammates. They are motivating and effective superiors. They are able to drive results irrespective of whether they are operating with a team of twenty or they are alone for three months on a project in an unknown land. They make the best partner for a CEO as his second-in-command. They are charismatic and inspiring leaders when they become CEOs themselves.

This is precisely the capability or skill you need to develop in yourself as you move forward towards your goal of becoming a *30-something CEO.* Irrespective of which company or industry you work for, your boss should love you and should be ready to do anything to never let you go. Your juniors should look up to you and aspire to be like you. Your teammates should have the faith that you would be willing to take a bullet for them.

Remember your career is like a race with many laps. You

cannot lag behind in some of them and then hope to dash and make-up in the last few. It doesn't work like that. Excellence and winning are both habits that need to be inculcated. You have to excel in each round. You have to be the best trainee when you start your career. You must get recognised as the top-performer when you are in active business. You ought to aim for that promotion before anyone else and get it. You've got to be the CEOs blue-eyed boy when you reach the senior rungs of management. It is only when you perform at every step, can you hope to become a *30-something CEO.*

You will see a winning entrepreneur has the ability to shut himself out and write a business plan all alone for weeks together. You will see the same guy lead a marketing workshop where he works closely with fifteen other people. You will also note that he will produce spectacular results in both the conditions. This is a specialty of most *30-something CEOs* – their output is not governed by their surroundings. It is the other way round.

7. The Juggler

> Either you run the day, or the day runs you.
>
> -Jim Rohn

If you have heard of the term 'multi-tasking', please know that fast-track achievers are a personification of this term. Someone who has not been on the other side of the table cannot even imagine the number of deliverables a true champion allocates to himself and the rigour with which he goes after them. I am here to take you to the other side of the table.

I once had the good fortune of meeting Sri Sri Ravi Shankar, the spiritual leader of millions and the Founder of the global 'Art of Living' network. From a distance, I would have expected to meet a soft-spoken *yogi* surrounded by a few disciples, leading a slow and quiet life. Well, I *did* meet a soft-spoken *yogi* – just that his disciples ran into millions and his life was anything but slow and quiet! We had been given only five minutes to meet him, at 8.45 pm sharp. When I reached the venue, I saw at least twenty other people waiting, each of them for their five minutes with *Guruji* (as Sri Sri is lovingly called). Finally, after a long wait we got our chance to meet him face to face. I was both nervous and delighted at the prospect of meeting one of the world's greatest spiritual leaders. My meeting with him was like a dream. We met, we spoke, he blessed us and we were out. I could see Guruji was visibly tired and yet in those counted minutes he had grasped the concept I wished to explain to him, advised us on the next steps and even stood up for a loving photograph with me that I requested him for. I left the room filled with awe and respect. I was blessed to have been able to spend time with him at such close quarters.

It was only after we stepped out that Guruji's team told us about his day. He had started from Bangalore at 4 am and flew to New Delhi. Thereon, he visited a riot-stricken district of the Indian state of Haryana and urged the public there to maintain peace. He then drove back to the National capital and attended meetings with senior government officials for a grand world culture festival that he was planning. He then came back to a bungalow at Golf Links where he was greeted by thousands of disciples and hundreds of people like me waiting to meet him. He attended to each one of us patiently and attentively. We were told his meetings will go on well into the night. I was stunned to see this 59-year-old working harder than the most hardworking CEO I had ever met, managing more things at a time than most super-achievers I have seen. As I was driving back from the venue I collected my thoughts about how Sri Sri started Art of Living at the young age of 24, and how his divine simplicity has led to Art of Living becoming a mammoth global organisation spanning over 150 countries. I just knew that instant. Guruji was a *30-something CEO*. I smiled at this crazy thought, but I felt even more connected with him.

> Time is the scarcest resource and unless it is managed nothing else can be managed.
>
> – Peter Drucker

Let's come back to the world of business. How do you think Sachin and Binny Bansal (Founders of Flipkart) must be spending their days? They are both literally *30-something CEOs*. Can you even imagine the innumerable matters that must be screaming for their attention on a daily and hourly basis? How does one manage a brilliant and massive company like Flipkart that has redefined retail in this country and has created history? What do you think it takes to lead an organisation that sells billions of products to millions of customers on its platform? Of course, they will have a fine team around them, but which end of the business do they focus on at what hour? The logistics involved in running a company like Flipkart is nothing short of being scary. The customer-facing processes must be totally unnerving. The brand management, the supplier-end, the competitive landscape, the technology infrastructure, the user-experience, the consumer analytics, the financial management... *gasp*! Even talking about it gives me the jitters. Now think about how Sachin and Binny must be running the show. Not just running the show, but driving Flipkart unstoppably towards becoming one of the most valuable companies in recent times. Needless to say, they are both jugglers par excellence. They are icons. They are *30-something CEOs*.

Multi-tasking is the most underrated quality in the industry today. It is also something most people assume they can do. Nothing could be farther from the truth. I have worked with several people during my career for whom multi-tasking became the biggest nemesis. They were very good performers as long as their scope of work was restricted to one or two responsibilities. As they grew in rank and role, they failed miserably! That was only because they could not manage the multiple expectations that came with the role.

The real problem with multi-tasking is that it is horribly

misunderstood. People feel that if they are attending meetings, responding to emails and visiting a client, all on the same day, they are multi-tasking. That is so not correct! Multi-tasking is not about doing many things one after the other. It is about doing them at the same time – *and delivering results in each one of them.* The second part of the statement is even more important because many times people feel that just because they are *involved* in many things simultaneously, they are multi-tasking. No they are not. Are they delivering the expected *output* in each of those tasks? That is the real test.

What is the difference between a super-computer and a regular PC machine? The answer lies in the processing power. The super-computer can process exponentially higher number of transactions per given unit of time as compared to the regular desktop. This is quite like the difference between a winner and a mediocre individual. A *30-something CEO* conditions himself over the years to be able to process and deliver on a much higher number of achievables than a regular worker.

I hope you noticed that I used the word 'conditions' in my last sentence. Yes, even this is an acquired trait. No one is born a multi-tasker. The same rules for the *30-something CEOs* to nurture creativity, apply for the art of jugglery or multi-tasking. It is only when you drive yourself to the hilt to deliver results on multiple fronts that you will actually learn to achieve it. Always keep checking with yourself – are you just 'active' or are you really productive? There is a big difference between being busy and being useful. It is only when you learn the art of not only managing many things together but also showing visible results on each, that you can call yourself a multi-tasker.

8. A broken record

> Only put off until tomorrow what you are willing to die having left undone.
>
> – Pablo Picasso

Did you notice when I was describing the trait of how most successful people are enthusiastic social animals, I wrote a sentence that said, "*They may or may not be universally popular…*"? There is a reason for saying this.

What is the one common thread between all high-speed winners? It is simple - they get the job done. No matter what. No matter how. They get it done. That does not make things most favourable for them when it comes to the popularity charts. They don't become everyone's favourites. I don't think they care, as long as they are building value for everyone.

The title of this section '*A broken record*' is what someone called me a few years ago. You do know what a broken-record is, don't you? It is a phrase used for someone who gets stuck on the same thing and keeps saying it over and over again. It is picked-up loosely from the term used to describe the musical record albums that would get stuck, skip back a moment and keep playing the same piece again and again. It is a phrase used mostly in a negative sense for someone who is annoyingly repetitive. Believe me, this repetitiveness works wonders in business.

Let me tell you how it was used for me. It was actually quite a funny incident. There was a massive automobile client that we had at our advertising business a couple of years ago. Since our agencies Magnon eg+ and Magnon\TBWA are among the finest digital agencies in India, I knew there was great potential in winning the digital end of the client's business as well. I would get on international conference calls with the global account director (GAD) of that client every alternate week. The GAD led our agency's global relationship with that client and I knew he was the best guy to show me the way towards winning the digital business too. We were both very interested in discussing the health of the advertising relationship as it was our largest client there, but it was frustrating to observe that as soon as the advertising discussion would end, he would scurry to end the call and avoid my queries on how we could pitch for the digital side of the business. It was probably an area he didn't want to commit himself to at that time, but then he was dealing with someone who was programmed to not let go.

As a few weeks passed, I got even more determined. The GAD and I had a lot of mutual respect and liking, and I did not want to disturb that at any cost. On the other hand, I had to get my point across. I had to get my answers. I had to win the digital business. This piece of business was going to be significant for our digital agency, and I had to press on. So I started asking about this matter at the end of every call. *Every* call. The first couple of calls the GAD dodged my questions as usual. But with every call he could sense my persistence. Till one day, he said in an exasperated tone, when I repeated my question about the digital business, *"Vineet aren't you one helluva broken-record about this point?"* We both shared a hearty laugh after which he gave me the critical advice and introductions I needed from him. We won the digital business within the next 45 days.

> Persistence is to the character of man as carbon is to steel.
>
> – Napoleon Hill

'Follow-up till it gets done' seems to be the motto by which most super-achievers live. They are champions of following-up. They follow-up with their seniors, juniors, clients, investors, suppliers, bankers… and just about everyone they deal with. They know human beings are programmed to prioritise *urgent* over *important*. And the surest way to get something done by someone is to move your task from their important list to their urgent list. And incessant follow-up does wonders for that.

A lot of my teammates used to hate me for it (they still do at some level I am sure). They despised the way I would get hooked on to something and then chase it like it was the only thing I had left to do during my visit to this planet. Gradually they started appreciating the effectiveness of this *modus operandi.* They could see how things would get done simply and simply because someone was not loosening the grip. Today, most of them have become like me and have mastered the art of follow-up. They are tremendously effective. Their teammates hate them for it!

Most people don't seem to fully understand the power and the importance of following-up if you want something done. Haven't we all heard so many times in office, *"I sent the mail but she didn't respond"* or *"I completed my part of the report but my team members did not"* or the classic one, *"I have sent him the mail twice but he has not got it done?"* God!

Let me tell you the difference between an ordinary worker and *the 30-something CEO*. The ordinary worker thinks getting work *off* his desk is his duty. The *30-something CEO* believes that getting the work *concluded* is his duty. The ordinary worker sends an email, passes the buck and forgets about the matter. *The 30-something CEO* sends the email, calls up the recipient, confirms receipt, discusses the next steps, shares a laugh and follows-up the next morning to make sure the task got completed.

The winners know they have to achieve a lot – every hour, every day... 24x7x365. They know there are many things that need to get done. They know only results count. They know things don't get done on their own. Most people don't progress work unless coaxed. They know even if it takes a hundred reminders to get something over the hill, it is worthwhile - because an inch covered by an industrious ant is more distance than what is covered by a mighty eagle sitting idle.

9. I believe I can fly

> All men's gains are the fruit of venturing.
>
> \- Herodotus

Ask any successful entrepreneur if he can send a man to Mars, trust me he will not say no. He will say he can do it, given the right investment, the right research and infrastructure and the right people. The sheer Herculean nature of the task at hand will not scare him, as long as he can see value-creation in it. He is a believer. In himself.

Although this is the last section of this chapter and the final common trait of *30-something CEOs* that we will be discussing, I have to say it is my absolute favourite. I purposefully kept it for the end. Without this one trait, everything else becomes meaningless. You may be phenomenally enterprising. Of what use is enterprise if it does not instil deep confidence and self-belief in you? You might be someone who is loved by his colleagues and teammates. However, if you don't have boundless faith in your own ability, what purpose will this fellowship serve? Remember this – you may be weak, under-prepared, lacking in resources, poorly qualified or whatever else. But if you believe you can achieve something despite all odds, you are half-way there! On the other hand, you might be an extremely capable individual, having all the right degrees, a great attitude and everything else. If that still leaves you doubting your own ability, it is all worthless.

Amelia Earhart flew across the Atlantic solo because she believed she could do it. Virender Sehwag completed his triple century twice because he trusted himself with getting the ball across the boundary every time he hit it. When brilliant engineers and management graduates from premier institutions of the country forego lucrative job offers and throw themselves into the start-up fray, they do so because they believe they will create great companies. Every time history has been written, it is because one human being decided to step out and take the big leap that no one else could imagine was possible. It could be man landing on the Moon or climbing the Everest, swimming the length of the mighty Amazon river or building a global company named after it – there is always self-belief at the core of every winning story. And that will be the deciding factor behind your story as well.

> If you set your goals ridiculously high and it's a failure, you will fail above everyone else's success.
>
> – James Cameron

You can do nothing unless you truly, from the bottom of your heart, the nucleus of your intellect and the depth of your soul, believe you can do it. A little bit of doubt is okay. In fact, it is healthy. It keeps you on your toes, avoids complacency and pushes you to prepare better. Anything more than that will forever hold you back from what you could have been. If you think you can build a billion-dollar company, you probably can. If you believe you can be the next big Vice President in your organisation, you are already half-way there. If you think you can become a famous painter, you've already made progress. Remember – once a thought is seeded in your mind, all it needs thereafter is nourishment from your own belief.

I heard this beautiful line from a little girl giving a lecture on living life to the fullest. She was terminally ill but spoke like she was the happiest person on Earth. It was one of the most profound speeches I have ever heard and her words ring in my heart even today. She said that every good thing in life happens twice. It first happens in the depths of your mind, before it happens again in reality. Think about it. Didn't your first kiss appear fuzzily in your head before it actually happened? Didn't you dream about driving that swanky car with your friends, first in your thoughts, before you went out and bought it? Didn't you imagine yourself working happily in the organisation that you finally got selected for? You see, everything that we cherish first takes place in our minds. And then something comes together between the fabric of our determination and the forces of the cosmos, which jointly convert that thought into reality.

So as I write this book, I am imagining its third print-run coming out with a 'National Bestseller' stamp on it. See? It has already happened once in my mind! I will now consciously and sub-consciously work towards making it a reality. All my actions, decisions and expectations will be governed by that best-seller dream that has already germinated deep down in my system. Do you think I have a higher possibility of becoming a best-selling writer now than when I never even thought about it? Today I believe I can do it. And it is not just about this book or writing. I am leading my company Talentrack with the intense belief that it will be a billion-dollar enterprise one day, counted among the largest brands in the media & entertainment industry worldwide. I drive my digital agency, Magnon with the ambition to grow it into one of the world's largest digital media companies. I have seen it all happening in my mind. I believe I can make it happen in reality.

All *30-something CEOs* share this self-belief. They are not afraid of dreaming and dreaming big. They allow themselves to spread their aspirational wings and aim for the stars. They don't fear the grind of the ride. They know the journey will be full of ups and downs, and they wire themselves to take it all in their stride. They know they will build the ship on the way, forging it slowly with the iron of their determination and the fuel of their sweat and blood.

With this, we conclude this book. I sincerely hope it has helped you spot opportunities both within and outside yourself. There may have been occasions during the chapters where you felt that I talk too much about the power people have over their destinies. You are probably right. I am someone who believes in the magic of human will, and have seen it build golden lives not once but many times. I am certain that there is a *30-something CEO* hidden inside all of us. Some of us are able to discover him within our working lives and as a result become extraordinary success stories. Unfortunately, most of us yearn for him with dry tears in our eyes as we rock helplessly on our retirement chairs many years down the line, not having lived even a tenth of the life we could have. This book has been a committed effort from me to help you find your hero within you, sooner than later.

Once again, *the 30-something CEO* is only a metaphor. It is what we all want to be in whatever we choose to do. As we have read earlier in the book, it does take some tricks and tactics, both good and bad, to become one. However, those tactics play a comparatively smaller role when it comes to the eventual emergence of *the 30-something CEO*. What makes the big difference – is you.

“Don't be dismayed by good-byes. A farewell is necessary before you can meet again. And meeting again after moments or lifetimes, is certain for those who are friends.

- Richard Bach

JAICO PUBLISHING HOUSE

Elevate Your Life. Transform Your World.

ESTABLISHED IN 1946, Jaico Publishing House is home to world-transforming authors such as Sri Sri Paramahansa Yogananda, Osho, the Dalai Lama, Sri Sri Ravi Shankar, Sadhguru, Robin Sharma, Deepak Chopra, Jack Canfield, Eknath Easwaran, Devdutt Pattanaik, Khushwant Singh, John Maxwell, Brian Tracy, and Stephen Hawking.

Our late founder Mr. Jaman Shah first established Jaico as a book distribution company. Sensing that independence was around the corner, he aptly named his company Jaico ('Jai' means victory in Hindi). In order to service the significant demand for affordable books in a developing nation, Mr. Shah initiated Jaico's own publications. Jaico was India's first publisher of paperback books in the English language.

While self-help, religion and philosophy, mind/body/spirit, and business titles form the cornerstone of our non-fiction list, we publish an exciting range of travel, current affairs, biography, and popular science books as well. Our renewed focus on popular fiction is evident in our new titles by a host of fresh young talent from India and abroad. Jaico's recently established translations division translates selected English content into nine regional languages.

Jaico distributes its own titles. With its headquarters in Mumbai, Jaico has branches in Ahmedabad, Bangalore, Chennai, Delhi, Hyderabad, and Kolkata.

SINCE 1946